NEW Streetwise

Upper Intermediate

Student's Book

OXFORD
UNIVERSITY PRESS

Rob Nolasco

Reading	Listening	Writing	Speaking
A questionnaire about teenage shopping habits	A programme about what shops do to make people buy things		Discussing shopping
A survey of teenage opinions about fast food			Discussing fast food and diets
A letter to a friend from American girl staying in England		A personal letter	Discussing the difficulties of living in a foreign country
	An interview with a mother studying in her daughter's class		Discussing whether older people should change and adapt
An article about how dolphins can help people with problems			Discussing if animals should be tourist attractions
		A letter of application	Discussing an advertisement
Two articles about a theme park accident			Discussing an imagined rescue
An article about Britain's naughtiest child			Discussing how to deal with naughty children
A story about a personal problem		A story	Discussing moral dilemmas
An article about young people's opinions of the Internet	A report about how computers could replace football referees		Discussing how computer technology affects the quality of life
Advice on how to do well in an interview	Listening to an expert on interviews		
A letter from an old lady about young people's behaviour		A composition about young people's attitudes	Discussing the generation gap
An article about people who believe we were visited by aliens	A personal account by a man who thinks he was kidnapped by aliens		Discussing alternative explanations of a kidnap story
An article about being left- and right-handed	A report on problems faced by left-handed people		Discussing discrimination against left-handers
	A film review of *Romeo and Juliet*	A film review	Discussing favourite types of film
An extract from the novel *Lord of the Flies*	A summary of what happened in *Lord of the Flies*		Discussing rules for survival
An article about how we feel about imitators			Discussing imitators
	Extracts from letters to problem pages	A letter asking for and giving guidance	Discussing a problem and giving advice

Reading	Listening	Writing	Speaking
Article about two complete strangers who get married	A report about marriage in the UK		Discussing what makes marriages work
An article about mixed and single-sex schools			Discussing gender and schooling
Descriptions of the same person by different people		A personal description	Discussing how you behave in different situations
An article about a moral dilemma	People talking about problem friends		Discussing what makes a happy friendship
An article about the effects of music			Discussing the effects of different kinds of music
An article about basketball fans		An article about an important national event	Discussing your favourite sports teams
An article about a polar explorer	A report about women explorers		Discussing whether the golden age of exploration has passed, is here, or is about to happen
An article about cycle helmets			Conducting a class survey
An article about changing attitudes in sport		An opinion piece (ideas for and against)	Discussing opinions on sport
An article about why people believe in horoscopes			Discussing graphology
An article about the benefits of a gap year	An interview with three people considering a gap year		
Report on pop music		A report on pop music	Discussing what kind of pop music you like
Two people's views about the same blind date			Discussing a blind date
	An interview with a woman who kick boxes		Discussing the suitability of violent sports for men and women
A story about a strange incident		Rewriting a story from a different point of view	
An article about a teenage inventor	An interview about strange inventions		Discussing your favourite invention
An article about television			Discussing what people do when watching TV
Opinions about city and village life		A description of the place you live in	Discussing the advantages and disadvantages of country and city life

OXFORD
UNIVERSITY PRESS

Great Clarendon Street, Oxford OX2 6DP

Oxford University Press is a department of the University of Oxford.
It furthers the University's objective of excellence in research,
scholarship, and education by publishing worldwide in

Oxford New York

Athens Auckland Bangkok Bogotá Buenos Aires
Calcutta Cape Town Chennai Dar es Salaam Delhi Florence
Hong Kong Istanbul Karachi Kuala Lumpur Madrid Melbourne
Mexico City Mumbai Nairobi Paris São Paulo Singapore
Taipei Tokyo Toronto Warsaw

with associated companies in Berlin Ibadan

Oxford and Oxford English are registered trade marks of
Oxford University Press in the UK and in certain other countries

ISBN 0 19 433409 0

First impression 2000

Printed in Hong Kong

Acknowledgements

The publishers would like to thank the following for their time
and assistance.
Galleria, Hatfield; The Hertfordshire & Essex High School; Virgin
Cinema, Harlow.

**The publishers would like to thank the following for their kind
permission to reproduce copyright material.**
Return To Sender (p 14) Words and Music by Otis Blackwell and
Winfield Scott © 1962 by ELVIS PRESLEY MUSIC, INC. administered
worldwide by Williamson Music, New York, USA. All Rights Reserved.
Lyric reproduction by kind permission of CARLIN MUSIC CORP.,
London NE1 8BD.
Eighteen (p 32) Words and Music by Alice Cooper, Michael Bruce,
Dennis Dunaway, Neal Smith and Glen Buxton © 1971 BIZARRE MUSIC
INC. AND EZRA MUSIC CORP. all rights administered by Bizarre Music
Inc. Copyright Renewed – All Rights Reserved. Lyric reproduction by
kind permission of CARLIN MUSIC CORP., London NE1 8BD.
Teenager In Love (p 50) Words and Music by: Doc Pomus and Mort
Shuman ©1962 by Unichappell Music, Inc. Copyright Renewed – All
Rights Reserved. Lyric reproduction by kind permission of CARLIN
MUSIC CORP., London NE1 8BD.
What Can I Do (Corr/Corr/Corr/Corr) (p 68) Lyrics © 1997 by kind
permission of Universal Music Publishing Ltd.

(Everything I Do) I Do It For You (p 86) Words and Music by Bryan
Adams, Robert John 'Mutt' Lange and Michael Kamen © 1991 by kind
permission of Universal Music Publishing Ltd. (62.50%), © 1991 Almo
Music Corp, Badams Music, Out Of Pocket Productions Ltd, Miracle
Creek Music and Zachary Creek Music (18.75%) Rondor Music (London)
Ltd, London SW6 4TW. Reproduced by permission of International
Music Publications Ltd.
Because You Loved Me (p 104) Words and Music by Diane Warren
© 1996 Realsongs, USA. 90% EMI Music Publishing Ltd, London WC2H
0EA. Reproduced by permission of IMP Ltd.

Cover illustration by
Arlene Adams

Illustrations by
Kathryn Adams pp 31, 42, 85, 91, 93, 114; Dominic Bugatto pp 12, 46,
96, 97, 102; Phil Healey pp 29, 35, 37, 47; Kveta Jelinek pp 10, 21, 67, 88;
Pantelis Palio pp 11, 20, 59, 108

Commissioned photography by
Trevor Clifford pp 7 (shoppers, girl with pen), 15 (mother & daughter),
16, 25 (Daniel & teens), 28, 32, 33 (male & teen with headphones), 43
(left-handed items), 61 (girl), 68, 70, 97 (date), 98, 105 (inventions), 107
(rollerblades), 110

**The publishers would like to thank the following for their kind
permission to reproduce photographs.**
Allsport pp 69 (Jamie Squire/basketball), 75 (Clive Brunskill), 97 (John
Gichigi/boxing), 101 (David Leeds/boxing), 101 (Gary M Prior/tennis),
101 (Matthew Stockman/basketball), 101 (Jed Jacobsohn/American
football); Associated Press AP pp 61 (mass wedding), 74; Christie's
Images p 78 (table); Corbis pp 7 (Bob Winsett/fast food restaurants), 69
(Paul A.Souders/ballerina), 111 (Gillian Darley, Edifice/apartments);
Fortean Picture Library pp 43 (Andy Radford/flying saucer), 44 (Klaus
Aarsleff/Petroglyphs), 45; Ronald Grant Archive pp 44 (Fire in The Sky),
48 (a, b, e, f, g, h, i), 51 (Lord of the Flies); Robert Harding Picture Library
p 17 (rollerblading); Houses & Interior p 78 (Jake Fitzjones/chair); IKEA
2000 p 78 (desk); Image Bank pp 17 (Yellow Dog Productions/ surfers),
18 (Jeff Hunter), 33 (Michael Coyne/girl at computer), 50 (David De
Lossy), 84 (Terje Rakke/tennis), 101 (John P.Kelly/golf); Images Colour
Library p 111 (bungalow); Katz Pictures pp 7 (James Leynse/SABA/food
stall & frankfurter store), 87 (Richard Baker/store); Courtesy Kobal p 43
(20th Century Fox/Merrick Morton/Romeo & Juliet), 48 (Miramax/d),
48 (United Artists/c), 52 (Castle Rock/Columbia Pictures); Network
p 111 (Gideon Mendel/ shanty hut); Nintendo p 107 (Gameboy); PA
News pp 26, 62, 79 (David Hempleman-Adams), 80 (climber); Pictor
p 104; Pictorial Press p 86 (Warner/Robin Hood); Powerstock Zefa pp 7
(Asian girl), 8 (girl), 24, 56, 61 (girls in uniform), 64 (science), 84 (coach
& boy), 105 (watching TV, Barcelona), 106 (male), 111 (manor house);
Project Trust pp 87, 90 (Dave Morgan, Liz Hopkins); Raleigh Industries
Ltd p 107 (mountain bike); Redferns pp 72 (E.R/quartet), 72 (Mick
Hutson/ Iron Maiden), 72 (David Refern/Jazz), 92 (Mick Hutson/Cast);
Retna pp 7 (Jenny Acheson/male), 8 (Michael Putland/male), 10 (John
Powell/male in dark shirt), 10 (Jenny Acheson/hippy girl), 10 (Ken
Bank/male), 38 (Phillip Reeson), 92 (Colin Bell/Five), 92 (Eddie
Malluk/B.Spears), 92 (Steve Double/rap band), 92 (Steve Granitz/
B*Witched); Rex Features pp 17 (judo), 25 (ride), 51 (Monroe
lookalikes), 54, 69 (Steve Lyne/exam), 80 (Action Sport/Breitling
balloon), 85 (Tony Larkin), 100 (Cooke); Science Photo Library pp 80
(Simon Fraser/snowy landscape), 87 (Jean-Loup Charmet/astrology);
SEGA Dreamcast p 107 (Dreamcast); SONY UK p 107 (CD Discman);
Tony Stone Images pp 14 (Dugald Bremner), (Kim Westerskov/
dolphins), 27 (Pete Seaward), 61 (Andy Sacks/mixed class), 66 (Jon
Riley), 79 (Joe McBride/skateboarder), 79 (Steven Peters/swimmer), 82
(Brian Bailey), 111 (cottage); Topham Picturepoint pp 9, 106 (Eddison);
John Walmsley pp 7 (girl), 64 (cookery)

NEW
Streetwise

Shopping — What do you buy when you go shopping?

Fast food — What do you understand by the term fast food?

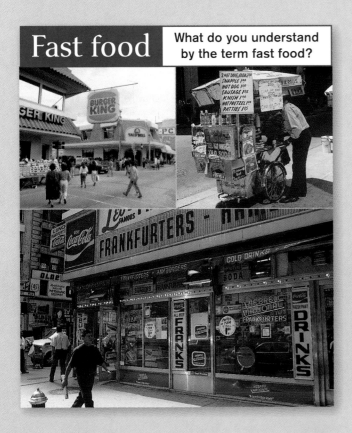

Yours — Would you make a good penfriend? Why/Why not?

Shopping

Warm-up

1 Are teenagers more fashion conscious than people of other ages? Why/Why not?

Reading

2 Complete the questionnaire, then answer these questions.

1 How many typical answers did *you* give?
2 Use your own words to describe the view of a typical teenager as suggested by the questionnaire.
3 Do you think that there is such a thing as a typical teenager? Why/Why not?

Are you a typical teenage consumer?

Answer the following questions and find out.

1 Are you fashion conscious?
The magazines are full of the latest fashions. Do you go straight to the shops to try them on?

a Yes. I always try my best to keep up with the latest styles.
b I'm quite interested, but wouldn't say I was clothes mad.
c No. Fashion doesn't interest me.

2 Will you pay extra for designer clothes?
You are in an exclusive shop when you find some jeans that you really like. There's no price on them, but on your way to pay you decide that if they're over £50 you'll ...

a ... have to put them back. There's no way you are going to spend so much money on one pair of jeans.
b ... buy them without thinking twice. It's worth spending a bit extra for better quality.
c You never go and pay if you don't know how much something is going to cost.

3 How do you usually spend your cash?
Someone has just given surprise gift of some money. What are you going to do with it?

a Go straight to the shops and buy something to wear.
b Save it for later.
c Buy some CDs or tapes.

4 Are you brand conscious?
Is there a difference between Pepsi Cola and Coca Cola?

a No. Colas are all the same.
b Yes, but I can't tell the difference!
c Yes. I only drink the one I like.

5 Are you an impulsive shopper?

a Yes. I love doing things without thinking about them.
b No. I rarely act without thinking.
c It depends. Sometimes I am, sometimes I'm not.

Today's 'typical' teenager would give the following answers:

1 Teenagers are over twice as likely as the rest of the population to describe themselves as fashion conscious. The typical answer is a.

2 A minority of teenagers said that they would buy designer clothes without thinking. The typical teenager does not have the money to worry about designer labels. The typical answer is a.

3 Teenagers spend most of their money on clothes. This is followed by albums and CDs and going out. The typical answer is a.

4 Teenagers are much more product conscious than adults. The typical answer is c.

5 Most teenagers would describe themselves as impulsive. The typical answer is a.

Vocabulary

3 Find words and expressions in the text which mean:

1 newest, most recent (l...)
2 if you always know about the latest fashions (f... c...)
3 expensive; limited to people who have a lot of money (e...)
4 without stopping to consider something (w... t... t...)
5 if you do things suddenly and without thinking (i...)

Practice

4 Think about your shopping habits. Use adverbs of frequency and appropriate present-tense verbs to write a paragraph describing them. First write and answer questions such as *Who do you go with? Where? When? How often? What do you buy? Are you impulsive?*, etc. Then summarize your answers in a paragraph describing your shopping habits.

Example
I love going shopping. I usually go with my friend Marc ...

Listening 📼

5 Next time you go shopping, look around. Shops have ways of getting you to spend money and you probably don't even notice. *New Streetwise* reports on what shops do to make us buy. Look at the sentences below. Try and guess the missing words before listening to the tape to check your answers.

1 Shops have w_____ doors to make you want to go in.
2 Music makes you feel r_____ and more likely to spend money.
3 In changing rooms mirrors and special lights can make you look healthy and s_____ .
4 Music or sports videos on banks of TVs make shopping more e_____.
5 What time is it? There are no c_____ on the wall so you don't worry about time.
6 Shops use smells to make us feel h_____ .
7 Cafes in the store give you a place to r_____ so you can shop some more.
8 Advertising is everywhere. On the f_____, on the walls. Everywhere!

6 Do you think shops in your country use these methods? In what ways is shopping in your country similar or different?

Fast food

Warm-up

1 How often do you eat fast food? What is your favourite? Do you ever think about how healthy your diet is?

Reading 📼

2 Read these teenagers' views on fast food and answer the questions.

1 Which of the speakers:
- is a fast food addict?
- does not eat meat?
- doesn't like the smell of sausages?
- thinks fast food tastes like plastic?
- is always hungry?
- is against American fast food restaurants?
- likes his Mum's cooking best?
- likes tomato sauce on everything?
- loves animals?

2 Is your opinion closest to Chloe's, Paul's or Wayne's? Are there any opinions that you strongly disagree with? Why/Why not?

Glossary

disposable: *something that is designed to be thrown away after being used*

I really hate all the American fast food restaurants that we have now. They all look the same, the food tastes like plastic, and although a burger and fries contains loads of calories, you are hungry again five minutes later. These companies waste a lot of paper and packaging as everything is disposable. Some of them have been blamed for the destruction of the Amazon rain forest too. I like a lot of traditional food. In fact I like my mum's cooking best.

Paul

I love fast food. My friends think I'm a fast food addict. Last Saturday I went out with some friends after a basketball match and I had two slices of pizza, a burger and fries, a hot dog, and two milkshakes. My friends think it's funny but my mum is a bit worried about my diet. I don't know why but I always feel hungry. I suppose I stay healthy because I play basketball every day. Anyway, I'm still growing so I need the energy. I do like other foods but only if they're covered in tomato sauce!

Wayne

I'm a vegetarian and I've been a vegetarian for two years now. I gave up meat because I love animals. I used to like steaks and sausages. In fact, hamburgers were my favourite food. Now I think that beef tastes like cardboard, and sausages and hamburgers smell disgusting. I can't even go into hamburger restaurants, because the smell makes me feel ill. I still eat fast food though. I love pizza, fries, baked potatoes, and salad in pitta bread. I think my diet is much healthier. I don't think you need to eat meat at all.

Chloe

Vocabulary

3 Match the adjectives to the foods in the pictures. You may use some more than once.

creamy   delicious   sweet   hot   bitter   salty   tempting   juicy   rich   nasty

yoghurt

lemon

potato crisps

red chillies

chocolate

Improve your grammar

feel, look, seem, smell, sound, taste

Verbs like *feel, look, seem, smell, sound,* and *taste* can be used with adjectives.

Example

The food tasted good. (= The food was good to taste.)

Not ~~The food tasted well~~.

Feel, look, seem, smell, sound, and *taste* can be followed by *like* + noun or *like* + adjective + noun.

Example

It looks like (tiny) doughnuts.

We do not usually use the progressive form with these verbs.

Example

It tastes horrible.

Not ~~It is tasting horrible~~.

We can use the progressive form when *feel* and *look* express the physical or emotional state of a person.

Example

I'm feeling sick/nervous/disappointed/etc.

Practice

4 Complete this review of a fast food restaurant using these verbs.

look   feels like   looks like   taste   smell

> ### Mr Fast
>
> This new chain of restaurants (1) __ any other fast food restaurant from the outside. However, inside you soon notice there are differences.   Mr Fast sells healthy, unusual, and tasty fast food. One of their most popular dishes is a roast beef sandwich with a spicy chilli sauce. You can (2) ___ these as you walk up the street. The sandwiches (3) __ delicious and (4) __ even better. The staff smile a lot and so it (5) __ a friendly place to eat.

5 Complete these sentences using verb + *like* + adjective or verb + adjective.

1 My favourite food _____.
2 I think hamburgers _____.
3 The fish market _____.
4 The music in the restaurant _____.
5 The pizza in the restaurant _____.
6 I _____ because of something I ate.
7 You _____.

Talking point

6 Work in small groups and discuss what you think of each of these statements. Be ready to share your views with the class.

1 Fast food is fattening and disgusting.
2 Food that is good for you is boring.
3 Vegetarians have healthier diets than meat-eaters.
4 You have to be on a diet to stay slim and healthy.
5 Young people pay too much attention to their weight.

Getting Streetwise! 📼

Compliments

7 It is polite to compliment people if they have made something for you, like a meal. However, you rarely compliment someone on something personal such as their hair, unless you know them well. Look at the picture. Would a compliment be appropriate in this situation in your country? What would you say?

8 You are going to hear four extracts of people giving and receiving compliments. Which of these expressions were used?

It really suits you.
You look well.
That was delicious.
You're so clever.

Listen again and decide on the situation in each extract.

9 Work in pairs. Compliment your neighbour on as many things as you can.

Yours

Warm-up

1 A friend of yours goes to live in another country and you decide to write. List the questions you would ask.

Examples
Have you made any friends?
Do you like the food?

Reading

2 Read this letter from an American girl in England to her friend at home and answer these questions.

1 How many of your questions from the Warm-up does the letter answer?
2 How has life changed for Nicole?
3 At what point does Nicole change the subject? How does she signal the change?
4 What is the function of the exclamations and underlining?
5 When do we use the abbreviation 'PS'?

Seaview
Vale Road
Torquay
Devon
TQ9 6HB

12 January

Dear Chelsea,

I know I should have contacted you before, but Mom and Dad have been really strict about the phone bill. I'm feeling a bit more settled now as we've been in England for almost six months although I miss you all a lot.

Last week, I had to give a presentation at school about being an American teenager in England. It was quite scary! I said that we don't use our car as much. Dad walks to the station to take a train to London and Mom cycles to work which she would never do back home. Having to wear a uniform feels weird and I miss wearing jeans and trainers to school. I still catch a bus to school. At the moment it's so cold and dark in the mornings that I find it hard to get out of bed. So some things never change. A lot of things are very different, the food, the way people speak, and yet it all feels the same too. I still go to school, do my homework, and hang out with friends. Maybe teenagers all over the world have things in common.

Anyway, I hope you are OK and are surviving Mr Heidelman's Geography class without me.

Please come and stay in the summer. My Mom is going to speak to your Mom about it. I can't wait!

I've got to go now as I've joined an exercise class with my new friend Charlotte. She's really cool, you'll like her. I'll tell you about her in my next letter.

Yours,

Nicole

PS Write and tell me all the gossip!

Vocabulary

3 Decide if these subjects are singular or plural.

1 my mom and dad
2 the weather
3 everyone
4 teenagers
5 nobody
6 the exercise class

4 Complete the sentences with the correct form of the verb.

1 There **is/are** a lot of people outside.
2 There **was/were** nothing in the box.
3 There **is/are** some eggs in the box.
4 There **was/were** no news.

Improve your writing

Writing a personal letter

a Put your own address in the top right-hand corner of the letter. You do not include the address of the person you are writing to in a personal letter.
Put the date under your address.
Examples
30th March 2000
30 March 2000   *30/03/2000*
These ways of writing the date are all acceptable.

b Put a comma after the greeting.
Example
Dear Isabella,

c The first sentence or paragraph introduces the letter and, if necessary, indicates why you are writing.
Examples
It was great hearing from you again ...
I thought I'd write to see how you are ...
I'm sorry I haven't written ...

d Use an appropriate style. Personal letters often include:
- contractions (*I'm* not *I am*)
- exclamation marks, underlining, etc., to make the letter more lively (*It's great!*)
- words like *well* or *anyway* to signal a change of topic.

e Round the letter off with a concluding paragraph.
Examples
(I) Hope to hear from you soon.
See you next week! (month/year/etc.)

f Sign off.
- *Best wishes* or *Yours* can be used in most informal letters.
- Use *Love* with close friends and relations.
- We normally use a comma after these expressions.
- *Yours sincerely* and *Yours faithfully* are used in formal rather than personal letters.
- x used at the end of a letter indicates a kiss.

Love,
Jake
xx

Practice

5 Choose the appropriate form. Give reasons for your answer.

1 We have been on holiday for a week now. I *stay/am staying* in a small hotel. I *go/am going* swimming most afternoons and we usually *spend/are spending* the evenings at a disco. I *have/am having* a great time.
2 I *write/am writing* to see if you can come to a party at my house on 18 July. I have decided to celebrate my sixteenth birthday, and I *hope/am hoping* you will be able to come.

6 Use the prompts to write a complete letter.

1 Thank/for/letter which reach me/Thursday
Thank you for your letter which reached me on Thursday.
2 I be glad/hear/you are well.
3 I just take/exams and I wait for/results.
4 My other news be/that/start/dancing lessons.
5 They be/great!
6 How about you? Do/still karate lessons, or you/give up?
7 Anyway, I want/invite you/a party next month.
8 The invitation/be enclosed.
9 hope/can come.
10 Well,/must run. I be late/a private lesson.
11 See/soon.

Talking point

7 How would life be different for a foreign family living in your country? Would it be easy for someone like Nicole and her family to settle in? Why/Why not?

Writing

8 Imagine Nicole's letter was addressed to you. Follow the *Improve your writing* guidelines and write a reply. In your reply you should:
- acknowledge her letter.
- give her the news about you and your family.
- talk about your recent activities, feelings, opinions, etc.
- respond to her invitation.
- bring the letter to a suitable conclusion.

Use as many of the words and expressions you have learnt in this issue as possible.

Self check

9 Read your partner's letter. Give them a mark for each piece of advice that they have followed in the *Improve your writing* section.

New Streetwise songbook

Return to sender 📼

Glossary

Return to sender: *an instruction written on a letter asking for it to be returned to the person who sent it*

Special D: *guaranteed quick delivery of your letter*

I (1) _____ (give) a letter to the post man,
He (2) _____ (put) it in his sack.
Bright and early next morning,
He (3) _____ (bring) my letter back.

She (4) _____ (write) upon it:
Return to sender,
Address unknown,
No such number,
No such zone.

We (5) _____ (have) a quarrel,
A lovers' spat,
I (6) _____ (write) 'I'm sorry',
But my letter (7) _____ (keep) coming back.

So when I (8) _____ (drop) it in the mailbox,
I (9) _____ (send) it 'Special D',
Bright and early next morning
It (10) _____ (come) right back to me.

She (11) _____ (write) upon it:
Return to sender,
Address unknown,
No such person,
No such zone.

This time I (12) _____ (take) it myself
   and put it right in her hand,
And if it (13) _____ (come) back the
   very next day
Then I (14) _____ (understand)

The writing on it:
Return to sender,
Address unknown,
No such person,
No such zone.

Return to sender,
Return to sender.

1 Do you write letters or send e-mails? Who do you write to?

2 Look at the verbs in the song and put them in the correct form.

3 Listen and check your answers.

4 What is the song about? What has happened?

5 *Mailbox* and *zone* are American English. What are they called in your language? What are they called in British English?

6 Discuss these questions in small groups:
• Do you think you can get to know someone or fall in love by letter or e-mail? Why/Why not?
• Do you think you could continue a relationship by letter or e-mail? How long for?

NEW
Streetwise

Class mates!

> Would you like to have your Mum or Dad in your school? Why/Why not?

Dear Sir/Madam

> What type of advertisement is this? Do you think this is a good advertisement? Why/Why not?

THE EUROPEAN PATENT OFFICE IN MUNICH

SEEKS TYPISTS

**to type from drafts
and audio tapes**

Minimum qualifications are secondary education, relevant professional training and experience, a working knowledge of one of the three official languages (English, French and German) and ability to understand another.

Applications (using forms available from the office) are to be submitted by 30th June 1993 to the European Patent Office, Personnel Department, Erhardstrasse 27, D-8000 Munich 2

Dolphin therapy

> What do you know about dolphins?

Class mates!

Warm-up

1 What do you think about adults going back to school to study?

Listening

2 Read the text and try to answer the questions. Then listen and check your predictions.

> Marian Morris is 42. Earlier this year she went back to school to do A level English. She shared a classroom with her daughter Katie, and *New Streetwise* interviewed them about the experience.

1 Which of these statements belong to Marian?
2 Which to Katie? Give reasons for your answers.

> 'If I go up to my bedroom and surround myself with books I think – Wow, I'm not doing the ironing or cleaning – this is my space.'
>
> 'Every time she opens her mouth I worry about what she's going to say and if she's going to make a fool of herself.'
>
> 'I've never felt embarrassed.'
>
> 'Every time she said something intelligent in class I wanted to clap.'
>
> 'The time she embarrassed me the most was when we were sitting in an exam working away and I smelled this funny smell. I looked over and she was pouring herself coffee.'

Vocabulary

3 Listen to the tape again, and explain the meaning of these phrases. Discuss your answers in pairs before using a dictionary.

1 a traffic jam
2 it only lasted a term
3 a mature person
4 gives me time off
5 that's worn off
6 I don't think I inhibit the girls
7 big enough to see

Pronunciation

Sentence stress

4 Listen and underline the words which are given greater stress than usual in these examples.

Katie do you have to ...?

I hadn't got A for anything before and I got three per cent more than Mum ...

This is something for me, if I go up to my bedroom and surround myself with books I think – Wow, I'm not doing the ironing or the cleaning – this is my space.

Why were these words stressed more than others?

5 Listen and repeat with the same stress and intonation.

Improve your grammar

Present perfect

a Look at these examples from the interview.
I have worked as a secretary for eighteen years ...
I'm older, I've read more books ...
Marian uses the present perfect simple to talk about her experiences up to the moment of speaking.

Present perfect simple and progressive

b Which example gives a greater sense of something continuing?
1 They have said the same thing for years.
2 They have been saying the same thing for years.

c Which example suggests that the activity is definitely over?
Which example suggests that the activity may or may not be over?
1 Marian has done her homework.
2 Marian has been doing her homework.

d Would you choose the simple or progressive form of the present perfect for these sentences. Why?
1 When are you going to stop? You _____ (read) all morning.
2 We _____ (read) four books so far this term.

Practice

6 Complete the sentences. Use the present perfect simple of these verbs.
read   work   play   win   live   go   swim
1 She __ as a secretary for eighteen years.
2 My uncle __ basketball for an American College team.
3 We __ in our house for years.
4 I __ Shakespeare's plays in my own language.
5 Mark has __ to Hawaii on holiday.
6 Tom Gregory __ the English Channel.
7 My team __ the national championship.

7 Complete the following sentences with the present perfect simple or progressive. Give reasons for your choice.

1 She (study) all day.
2 Why is the pillow so wet? I think she (cry).
3 How long (you learn) English?
4 Can I borrow your book? Sure, I (finish) it.
5 This book is very boring. I (only read) ten pages this week!
6 What (you think) about?
7 I'm sorry. I (forget) your name.
8 The bus is very late. We (wait) for an hour.

8 Put the verbs in brackets in an appropriate tense.
My name __ (be) Katie Morris. I __ (be) seventeen. I __ (go) to the Green School in north London for three years. My subjects __ (be) A level Literature, Sociology, and Mathemetics. For the last year my mother __ (do) A level Literature too. She is a good student. I think she __ (read) more books than me this term. I don't mind having her in my class, although she __ (embarrass) me on a number of occasions. The worst was when she __ (start) eating during a test. She __ (work) very hard so far, so I __ (hope) she __ (get) good marks in her exams.

Talking point

9 Which point of view do you share? A or B? Why?
Do you think that older people change and adapt? Does it matter if they don't? Do you think more of them should behave like Marian's mother? Why/Why not?

A
I think we should always respect what older people say. After all, they've seen more, read more, done more. They have a lot to teach us.

B
I don't see why we should automatically respect older people. They may have been around longer, but many of them have been saying and doing the same things for years. They don't have much to say about the world today.

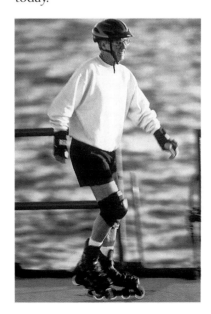

Dolphin therapy

Warm-up

1 Look at the picture. What is the woman doing? Would you like to try it? Why/Why not?

Reading 📼

2 Read the article and decide if these statements are true or false.

1 Matt Lindberg had a difficult childhood.
2 He wanted to swim with dolphins.
3 He met a dolphin and her baby.
4 The dolphin didn't like him.
5 He felt different after the swim.
6 Robert Slade's job is to study dolphins.
7 Slade believes dolphins can change our bodies.
8 Slade hopes to create a business like Dolphin Mania so that lots of people can swim with dolphins.
9 Slade believes that the mother dolphin wanted to harm Matt.

Vocabulary

3 Find words or expressions in the text that mean:

1 forced to leave (a school) (e...)
2 process of returning someone to a good way of living (r...)
3 area of sea water separated from the sea (l...)
4 treatment to improve your mental or physical health (t...)
5 very strong (i...)
6 get good effects from (b...)
7 animal kept with limited ability to move freely (i... c...)
8 living independently of people (i... t... w...)

Matt Lindberg is from Miami in the USA. Matt's mother left home when he was three and his father was an alcoholic. Matt was a very difficult child who was always in trouble. When he was 15, Matt was expelled from school, and when he was 16, he was arrested for stealing a car. Today, Matt is 20 and is a hard-working student at Florida State University. The change in Matt's behaviour came as a result of an unusual experience.

'I was taken to swim with dolphins as part of my rehabilitation after I had been arrested. I didn't really want to do it. When I was in the water a mother dolphin and her calf swam up to me. I felt their energy pass through me and we swam and played together. She had intelligent eyes. It was amazing. As I left the pool I felt at peace for the first time in my life.'

Matt went to Dolphin Mania, a special lagoon for swimming with dolphins in Florida. For most people, Dolphin Mania is a bit of holiday fun. For Matt, the experience changed his life. So what happened in the water?

Robert Slade is a computer scientist who lives in the Gulf of Mexico. He spends most of his free time swimming with dolphins and studying dolphin therapy. He has measured the changes in the brain waves of people who have swum with dolphins and he is sure that the dolphin's sonar can cause our body to change. He explains:

'The dolphin's sonar produces an intense amount of energy. This energy changes people so they become very relaxed. One day we hope to create this energy on a computer so people can benefit from it without keeping the dolphins in captivity. I would like to see all dolphins back in the wild.'
Slade witnessed Matt's swim with the dolphins. 'I think the mother was curious about Matthew in case he wanted to harm them. But when she played with Matt she found that he was really a gentle person inside.'

Glossary

sonar: *something that uses sound waves to discover the position of objects in the water*

Talking point

4 Work in small groups. What do you think of tourist attractions such as swimming with dolphins. Which of these statements do you agree with most? Why?

1 I think it is a way of exploiting animals to make money.
2 I think it encourages us to protect animals like dolphins.
3 Wild animals should be left in the wild and not be kept in captivity

Improve your grammar

Match the uses of the definite and zero articles to the examples.

a Definite article

1	the dolphin and the whale	a	with singular countable nouns when they stand for a species
2	the dolphin with her calf	b	with names of rivers, oceans and seas
3	the longest	c	with the names of places that include *of*
4	the South Seas	d	when it is clear that there is only one
5	the Gulf of Mexico	e	with superlatives

b Zero article

1	dolphins are mammals	a	names of most towns, cities and countries except for *the United States*, *the United Kingdom*, etc.
2	Florida	b	with plural countable nouns when making a general statement
3	can make money	c	with mass nouns when making a general statement

c A/an

1 What is the difference between:
Give me an apple.
Give me the apple.
2 Would you use *a* or *an* for these words?
apple, orange, banana, hour, holiday

Practice

5 Complete the following sentences with either *a/an*, *the*, or – (= zero).

1 Why are thousands of _____ dolphins dying?
2 _____ United States and _____ Canada have banned _____ drift nets from their waters.
3 It is wrong to keep _____ dolphins as _____ tourist attraction.
4 I think dolphins are _____ most beautiful animals in _____ world.
5 _____ whale oil is sometimes used for making _____ candles, _____ margarine, and _____ soap.

Pronunciation

6 When is *the* pronounced /ðə/?
When is *the* pronounced /ði:/?

1 the world   4 the air we breathe
2 one of the dolphins 5 the time
3 the environment

Listen and check your answers before repeating the phrases.

Getting Streetwise!

Making and responding to suggestions

7 A group of young people are discussing what they can do to help protect dolphins. Listen and tick the expressions they used to introduce the suggestions.

Let's ...
For a start we could ...
Why don't we ...
We might ...
We could ...
Do you think we should ...
Do you think we might ...
It might be an idea ...

8 Listen again. Decide if these reactions were positive, negative, or neutral.

That's a good idea!
Do you really think that would work?
What good would that do?
Why not?
I suppose you're right.
Now you're talking.

9 Work in small groups. Use these expressions in a discussion about an environmental issue you are interested in.

Dear Sir/Madam

Warm-up

1 Read the advertisement on the cover of this issue. What would you expect to find in a reply?

Reading 📼

2 Now read a reply to the advertisement and decide what is inappropriate about it. How can it be improved?

> Walnut Tree Cottage
> School Lane
> Foston
> Lincs NG32 2IG
>
> Personnel Department
> European Patent Office
> Erhardstrassa 27
> Munchi
>
> Dear sir or madam,
>   Pleas cosider me por the fost of typist what you want. I spotted youer ad in the Gradian today. I'm keen to get out of england and I'm told that Munchi is a good place to hide in.
>   I'm not bad at ptying as I've nearly finished my typing course at nightschool. I may need a dictionry though.
>   Can you let me know about the job as soon as possible because if you want me I'll finish this typing course right away and save some cash.
>   Yours faithfully,
>
>   Rick Crowe

Improve your writing

Writing a letter of application

a Make sure that you use an appropriate layout by organizing what you want to say in this way.

b Use the first paragraph to state your reason for writing. If you are replying to an advertisement you should always mention where you saw it.
Examples
I am writing in response to your advertisement in ...
I wish to apply for the position of ... which was advertised in ...

c Say more about your reason for writing in the main body of the letter. Draw attention to what makes you a particularly suitable applicant for the job/post/scholarship/course, etc.

Use present tenses to highlight your present situation/skills.
Examples
I am X years old ...
I speak fluent German and good French.

Use the present perfect/present perfect progressive to describe relevant recent or continuing experience.
Examples
I have recently left school and I am a student at a Technical College where I have been doing a typing course ...
I have been using a word processor since I was thirteen.

Use the past tense to describe relevant achievements in the past.
Examples
When I was fourteen I was in the school quiz team.
When I was at school I worked on the school newspaper.

Don't use contractions like *I'm, he's, they're* or informal expressions such as *Write soon* in formal letters.

d Conclude your letter. If appropriate, state what you want or what you hope will happen next.
I hope you will consider me for (the post/the scholarship/the course).
I look forward to hearing from you.

Practice

3 Complete the sentences to write a complete letter in reply to this advertisement.

> **Young person**
>
> with musical skills required to assist on nationwide summer courses for young children.
>
> **No experience required.**
>
> *Write to ...*

Dear Sir

I see/your advertisement/Issue 2 of *New Streetwise/* write in/hope that you consider/me for/job as a course assistant this summer.
I be 17/and study for/school-leaving exams.
I play/piano for seven years and recently pass/my advanced exams.
I always love/children, and last year I look after/two children/a month.
I not have/any experience of working/a course, but I help/in my uncle's shop since I be/sixteen, so I be/ reliable and hard-working.
I always want/to work with children, and I be/very happy/join your team.
I look forward/hear from/you.
Yours faithfully

Vocabulary

4 Work in small groups.
1 Look at the list of qualities commonly found in job advertisements. Make sure you know what each of these means. Can you add any more?

experienced   enthusiastic
sociable   hard-working
highly motivated   honest
confident   caring   flexible

2 Decide which qualities are important in these jobs.
a computer operator
a flight attendant
a police officer
a hospital doctor

Writing

5 Follow the *Improve your writing* guidelines and write your own letter of application for Small World's international scholarship. Invent any details required. Make sure you draw attention to your personal qualities.

Example
I am enthusiastic and hard working.

It's a small world

Small World is an international charity that offers young people a chance to live and study in a country of their choice.

Apply for your scholarship now!

Tell us about yourself and give us some idea of what you want to do and why.
If your letter is chosen, we will invite you to an interview and discuss your application further.

Write to: Mike Swallow, International Scholarships, Small World, World House, Trafalgar Square, London W1X

Self check

6 Work in small groups and read some of the letters of application. Decide on the best one. Check that the writer:

1 has included what the advert asked for.
2 did not make any serious grammar mistakes.
3 followed the rules for presenting this type of letter.

Grammar review

Issues 1 and 2

Present tenses

In English, we can use the simple present and the present progressive to talk about the present.

Uses	Examples
1 Simple present: for something which happens regularly, or to talk about habits.	*He works in an office.* *I often chew my nails.*
2 Simple present: to express a present state or general truths.	*I'm hungry.* *Do you like Beethoven?* *The sun rises in the east.*
3 Simple present: to describe present events in commentaries, demonstrations, etc.	*Erik passes the ball to Anderson, who shoots ...* *You beat the eggs and add them slowly ...*
4 Present progressive: to talk about events happening now.	*I'm washing my hair.* *It's raining.*
5 Present progressive: to talk about a temporary habit. Use *always* to show annoyance.	*I'm learning English.* *She's always speaking on the phone.*

Notes
We can also use present tenses to tell stories or jokes. This has the effect of making them more lively.
A woman is walking home. Suddenly she sees ...
For present tenses with future meaning (see page 36).

Non-progressive verbs

Some verbs are not normally found in progressive forms. These generally express a state rather than an action:
1 verbs of feelings/emotions, e.g. *like, love, hate*
   I like going to the cinema.
2 verbs of perception, e.g. *feel, hear, smell, see*
   That smells nice.
3 verbs of opinions, e.g. *think, know, appear, seem*
   I think you are wrong. I know her very well.

Note
Some of the verbs listed can be used in progressive forms when they are used with a different meaning. Compare:
She thinks you are right. (= opinion)
She's thinking about it. (= trying to make a decision)

Adverbs of frequency

These answer the question *How often ...?*
- *always* (i.e. all the time)
- *almost always, nearly always*
- *generally, normally, regularly, usually*
- *frequently, often*
- *sometimes, occasionally*
- *almost never, hardly ever, rarely, seldom*
- *not ... ever, never* (i.e. none of the time)
Adverbs of frequency usually go before the main verb.
I often feel hungry in the afternoon.

Verbs of perception

Uses
1 Verbs like *feel, look, seem, smell, sound* and *taste* can be used with adjectives.
   The food tasted good. (= The food had a nice taste.)
   That looks very nice.

2 *Feel, look, seem, smell, sound* and *taste* can be followed by *like* + noun (or adjective + noun).
   She sounds like Madonna.

Note
When they express a continuing perception we do not use the progressive form.
It tastes horrible. (**Not** ~~It is tasting horrible~~.)

When *feel* and *look* express the physical state of a person we can use the progressive.
I'm feeling sick/nervous/disappointed/etc.

Present perfect

The present perfect links the past and the present.

Uses	Examples
1 For actions which began in the past and still take place or are happening now.	*She has worked as a secretary for ages.* *I have lived here all my life.*
2 To relate experience (from the past up till now).	*Have you ever been to the disco? I've never seen you there.*

Note
A sentence like *I've seen this film* refers to a past action, but the time of the action is unspecified. If you want to specify the time of the past action you must use the simple past – *I saw this film last week.*

Present perfect simple and progressive

1 We use the present perfect progressive to emphasize the duration of an action (i.e. how long).
I've been doing this all morning.

We use the present perfect simple to talk about what has been achieved (i.e. finished in a period of time).
I've done two exercises this morning.

2 When we use the present perfect progressive, the action may or may not be finished. The emphasis is on the action.
I've been cleaning my guitar.

When we use the present perfect simple the action is finished. The emphasis is on the result.
I've cleaned my guitar.

Note
With the verbs *work* (= have a job) and *live* you can use either form with little difference in meaning.
He has lived/has been living here for years.

Indefinite article (*a/an*)

Uses	Examples
With singular countable nouns:	
1 for a general meaning (meaning 'any, it does not matter which').	*Give me an eraser.*
2 with a noun mentioned for the first time.	*There was a dog outside. The dog was very large.*
3 with numbers (e.g. *a hundred*) and fractions (e.g. *a quarter*).	*There were a million people in Trafalgar Square.*
4 to describe somebody's job or situation.	*My uncle is a doctor. My grandmother is a pensioner.*

Note
an is used before a word that begins with a vowel sound. Compare *an hour* /ən aʊə(r)/ and *a house* /ə haʊs/, *an MP* /ən empiː/ and *a mouse* /a maʊs/, *an umbrella* /ən ʌmbrelə/ and *a university* /ə juːnɪvɜːsətɪ/.

Pronunciation
a is normally pronounced /ə/.
an is usually pronounced /ən/.

Definite article (*the*)

The can combine with singular countable, plural countable, and uncountable nouns.

Uses	Examples
1 With singular countable nouns when they are an invention or species.	*He invented the telephone. The dolphin is an endangered species.*
2 With names of rivers, oceans and seas.	*The Amazon is the biggest river in the world.*
3 With the names of places that have *of*.	*I went to visit the Tower of London.*
4 When it is clear that there is only one.	*'Who's that at the door?' 'It's the postman.' Ann is in the garden.*
5 With superlatives.	*'She's the best!'*
6 With certain time expressions.	*'I'll see you in the morning.'*
7 With a unique object or group of people.	*The earth is round. The Jacksons are great.*
8 With a noun that becomes definite by being mentioned a second time.	*He stole a car. The car he stole was a Rolls Royce.*

Pronunciation

The is pronounced /ðə/ before consonant sounds and /ðiː/ before vowel sounds.
We can draw attention to a noun by using /ðiː/ to mean the one and only, or the main one.
He is the person to speak to.

Zero article

In some cases no article is necessary.

Uses	Examples
1 With names of towns, cities, and countries.	*Canberra is the capital of Australia.*
2 With plural countable nouns when making a general statement.	*Dolphins and whales are mammals.*
3 With uncountable nouns when making a general statement.	*Oil is a very important resource.*
4 With names of meals.	*Breakfast is served.*

Note
The exceptions to point 1 above include countries whose names include nouns like *Republic*, e.g. *the United Kingdom, the Irish Republic*, and plural forms such as *the United States, the Canary Islands*.

Grammar practice

A

1 Complete the sentences with the simple present or the present progressive form of the verb in brackets.

Example
I *am doing* (do) my homework. Can you answer the door?

1 'Where's Alan?' 'He _____ (sleep)'.
2 It never _____ (rain) in August.
3 What _____ he _____ (do)? I can't see him.
4 I normally _____ (go) to work at this time.
5 She _____ always _____ (pull) my hair.
6 Please make the tea. The water _____ (boil).
7 _____ you _____ (understand) him?

2 Read this interview with an English teacher and choose the correct form.

A How long **have you been/were you** teaching at this school?
B **I've been here/I am here** for four years.
A I see. Where were you before that?
B I **worked/have worked** in a school in Spain.
A Really? How long **have you been/were you** in Spain?
B About three years. I **liked/have liked** it but I **decided/have decided** to move to a better job.

3 Complete the sentences with *a/an*, *the*, or zero (-).

1 What time do you go to ____ work?
2 Do you often lie in ____ sun?
3 Who is ____ best singer in ____ world?
4 There were two people in the room, ____ man and ____ woman.
5 Last year I visited ____ China and ____ India.
6 What do you have for ____ lunch?
7 Have you ever seen ____ elephant in the wild?
8 Why is ____ letter 'E' lazy?
Because it is always in ____ bed!

B

1 Complete the dialogue.

A What is your favourite breakfast food?
B Rice crispies.
A What (1) _____ like?
B They're made from grains of rice.
A Ugh! That sounds (2) _____ .
B They're not! They're nice and crisp.
A What do they (3) _____ ?
B They don't have a strong taste. You need to add milk and sugar. When you do they make a noise.

A What does (4) _____ ?
B It's a popping sound.
A How (5) _____ eat them?
B Every day!
A You must like them.
B I do. (6) _____ great when I eat them.

2 Complete the sentences with the present perfect simple or progressive. Give reasons for your answers.

1 He's a good friend. I _____ (know) him for years.
2 Who _____ (eat) my sweets? The packet is almost empty.
3 'What's up?' 'I _____ (lost) my keys.'
4 He _____ (do) karate for years.
5 Bill _____ (leave) his old job. He _____ (work) in the United States for about three weeks now.
6 I'm afraid I can't play. I _____ (broke) my leg.

3 Complete the text with either *a/an*, *the*, or zero (-).

Panda facts
There are probably fewer than 1,000 wild pandas left in (1) ____ China. (2) ____ pandas used to be hunted, but that's been stopped. (3) ____ Chinese government has set up twelve special areas for (4) ____ pandas but their numbers are still falling. In (5) ____ 1980 (6) ____ World Wildlife Fund and (7) ____ People's Republic of China started (8) ____ project to learn more about (9) ____ giant panda. (10) ____ project was run by Western and Chinese scientists and they helped supply (11) ____ information to raise (12) ____ pandas in (13) ____ zoos outside (14) ____ China. A few years later (15) ____ baby panda was born in Madrid Zoo.

C

1 Write a short description of the sounds, smells, tastes, and sights that you associate with a trip or journey that you make regularly. (e.g. a regular visit to the countryside, the trip to and from school, etc.) Use mainly present tenses.

2 Write fifteen questions that you would like to ask one of your teachers about their career, life, and interests.

Rescue

What is the most frightening fun-fair ride you have been on?

The naughtiest child?

Are boys naughtier than girls?

Suspicion

Have you ever suspected a friend of doing something wrong? What did you do?

Rescue

1 What is happening in the photograph? How would you feel if you had to be rescued in this way? Share your answers with the class.

Reading 📼

2 Read one of the news reports as quickly as possible to find the answers to these questions.

1 Where and when did the problem occur?
2 How were the people rescued?

Alton Towers rescue

A woman escaped by rope from a cable car stranded over a 30m ravine at the Alton Towers amusement park yesterday.

She was among 28 people who were rescued from three cars after the one in which she was riding became tangled with a cable in high winds. A computerised safety system halted the 40-car ride, and some passengers were trapped for more than two hours.

Luckily, the emergency services had practised the same rescue at Alton Towers two weeks before, with staff acting as trapped passengers.

A man in a wheelchair was lowered to safety by firemen, who got to the car with special equipment.

From The Guardian newspaper

27 Saved in cable car terror

Cable car traps tourists

The thrill of the fair turned to terror for 27 tourists on a cable car yesterday. Terrified passengers were stranded above a 30m ravine for an agonizing two hours after their cable cars had come to a halt at Britain's biggest amusement park.

A small child who clung desperately to his rescuer was among the frightened holidaymakers who had to be lowered by ropes in the strong winds.

His mother burst into tears as they were reunited in the ambulance.

Rescue hero Mark Symonds had to crawl along the cable to reach the cars. He battled with high winds to climb down a ladder into the stranded cable car.

Mark, 25, said afterwards: 'The people inside were obviously very relieved to see me.'

One girl said: 'I thought we'd never get down. I kept thinking we were going to die.'

From The Daily Mirror newspaper

Glossary

ravine: *very deep, narrow, steep-sided valley between hills or mountains.*

the emergency services: *the fire brigade, police and ambulance service*

clung desperately: *held on tightly*

3 Read the reports more carefully and answer these questions

1 Why did the cable cars stop?
2 How were the passengers rescued?
3 Are there any factual differences between the two reports?
4 *The Guardian* is a 'quality' newspaper. *The Daily Mirror* is a 'popular' one. Compare the two reports. Think about:
• the difference in length
• the difference in vocabulary (which report used the most adjectives?)
• the information that is included or excluded
5 Is the story told in the order in which it happened? Why/Why not?

Vocabulary

4 Match the words and expressions.

1 tangled	brought together
2 thrill	causing great worry
3 stranded	excitement and pleasure
4 agonizing	unable to escape
5 burst into tears	twisted in an untidy way
6 reunited	started crying

5 Write explanations for these words and phrases from the text.

1 had come to a halt
2 high winds
3 battled

Pronunciation 📼

6 Read and listen to part of the text from *The Daily Mirror*. Then listen to the same passage broken up into short phrases. Try and repeat what you hear with the same word-linking and intonation.

Improve your grammar

Past tenses

a Look at the texts and find examples of the following:
• an irregular simple past
• the past progressive
• the past perfect
• the past passive

b When do we use the past perfect rather than the simple past?

c When do we use the past progressive rather than the simple past?

d Why is the passive often used in news reports?

Practice

7 Read this news report and put the verbs in brackets into the correct form.

Paolo Cesar (1) _____ (buy) a new sports car to (2) _____ (take) his fiancée for a holiday in the Swiss Alps. They (3) _____ (enjoy) the mountain scenery when suddenly they (4) _____ (surround) by thick fog. They soon (5) _____ (become) lost, (6) _____ (take) the wrong road and (7) _____ (drive) off the edge of a steep ravine.

Paolo and his girlfriend (8) _____ (injure). The car (9) _____ (damage). They (10) _____ (want) to light a fire but most of the petrol (11) _____ (leak) away. Quick thinking Paolo (12) _____ (remove) one of the magnesium wheels from his car. When he (13) _____ (hear) a helicopter, Paolo (14) _____ (throw) the remaining petrol on the wheel and (15) _____ (set) fire to it. The helicopter crew (16) _____ (see) the fire and (17) _____ (take) them to hospital where they had their injuries treated.

The naughtiest child?

Warm-up

1 Do you know any young children who are very naughty? What are some of the worst things they have done?

Reading 📼

2 Read this article about Britain's naughtiest child. How does he compare with any naughty children you know?

Watch out! Daniel's about!

Daniel Brown was just five years old when he climbed into the family car and let it roll away down the road. He was only three when he flooded the kitchen.

His mother, Angela Brown, is in despair. She is very busy looking after her new baby, a little girl called Laura, as well as Daniel. She told us, 'Daniel is so full of curiosity'. At that moment, we hear a huge crash and then silence. We go upstairs and find Daniel crawling out of a wardrobe he has pulled over onto the floor, with a book in his hand. 'It's for you Mum,' he says and looks up at his mum and smiles.

Seven-year-old Daniel has an angelic face. He has golden hair, big brown eyes, and a wide friendly grin. I have to admit that Daniel doesn't look like a naughty boy.

Angela told me all about it. 'Once I found him as he was about to put Jasper in the washing machine.' Jasper, she explained, is the Browns' dog. 'When I asked him why, he said that he thought Jasper was dirty! It's amazing how one little boy can cause so much trouble. Another time he cut off all the hair of the little girl next door. She was going to be a bridesmaid at her sister's wedding and the neighbours haven't spoken to us since.'

Angela told me about Daniel's most expensive crime. 'I was about to do the washing up when the baby started crying. Daniel decided to help and filled the kitchen sink with water. When I came in the water was already flooding the kitchen and was about to flood the hall. The carpet was ruined and had to be replaced. I hope things will get better as he gets older.'

Amazingly, Daniel is quite well behaved in school. This may be because he is rarely bored. Meanwhile he continues to be the naughtiest little boy in England. Will his baby sister Laura grow up to be the naughtiest little girl?

Glossary

angelic: *looking or seeming like an angel*

bridesmaid: *girl who carries the bride's flowers at a wedding*

full of curiosity: *wanting to know about everything*

3 Look back at the text and answer the questions.

1 Does Daniel look naughty or not?
2 What did he do while the reporter was talking to his mum?
3 In your opinion, which was the worst 'crime' mentioned in the text?
4 Why do you think he is so naughty?
5 Did you do anything very naughty when you were younger? What?

Vocabulary

4 What is the meaning of these words and phrases from the text?

1 grin
2 huge
3 crawling
4 curiosity
5 flood
6 crash

What is the meaning of the expressions in **bold**?

1 I used to **get away with** a lot because I was the youngest child
   a steal
   b escape unpunished
2 My father used to punish me but my mum often used to **let** me **off**.
   a not oblige someone to do something
   b give someone less punishment than they expected or none at all
3 My sister and I **fell out** when she discovered that I had read her diaries.
   a stop being friends, quarrel
   b drop out of something
4 **I get on with** my brothers and sisters.
   a have a friendly relationship with
   b make progress with

Improve your grammar

Future in the past

The future in the past can be expressed by *was going to* or *was about to*.

a These forms can refer to events which were planned to take place, and which did take place.
   Example
   Another time he cut off all the hair of the little girl next door. She was going to be a bridesmaid at her sister's wedding.

b They can refer to events which were intended, but which did not happen at the time because something interrupted or prevented them.
   Example
   'I was about to do the washing up when the baby started crying.' (So I didn't start.)
   In sentences like *I was going to see him* or *I was about to see him* we need further information to know whether the meeting took place or was prevented.

Practice

5 What was Daniel about to do? Use *was about to* and *was going to* to make sentences about each of the situations in the pictures.

   Example
   Daniel was about to put the dog in the washing machine when his Mum stopped him.

6 Imagine that you were also very naughty when you were younger. Look at the pictures and use the structures in the *Improve your grammar* box to write five sentences about some of the things you were going to do when you were interrupted.

Getting Streetwise! 📼

Expressing opinions

7 Listen to what Daniel's father says and tick the expressions he uses to express his opinions.

   I think ...
   If you ask me ...
   In my opinion ...
   According to ...
   As far as I'm concerned ...
   It's possible that ...
   I believe ...
   I suppose ...

8 Listen again and answer these questions.

1 In what ways do Daniel's mother and father treat him differently?
2 In what ways were his opinions the same or different from what you expected?

Talking point

9 Do you think you should punish a child like Daniel? How? Who do you think has the right idea, his mum or his dad? How would you deal with a naughty child?

Suspicion

1 Are you honest? What would you say to a friend if:

1 you thought your friend was responsible for stealing things in class?
2 you saw their boyfriend/girlfriend going out with someone else?
3 they were wearing something that looked really horrible on them?

Reading

2 Read this letter to a problem page and answer the questions.

1 Why is the writer worried about her friend Charlotte?
2 What would you do if you were the writer? How would you solve this dilemma? Would you:
- talk to the boss? Why/Why not?
- talk to your friend? Why/Why not?
- talk to the other staff? Why/Why not?
3 Use your own words to explain the writer's dilemma.

Suspicion

I work in a bakery on Saturdays. One day last week, our boss called all the staff into his office. Money was missing from the till and suddenly we were all under suspicion.

I didn't know what to think. You see, a vacancy came up two months ago and I persuaded my boss to give the job to Charlotte.

Everything was fine for the first few weeks. Charlotte liked the job and the boss was pleased with her. She even bought me a video as a thank you present for getting her the job.

I have always trusted Charlotte up till now but recently I've been worried about her. The thing is, the three other girls who work there apart from Charlotte have been there as long as me, and there's never been a problem.

In the last few weeks, I've noticed that Charlotte has been spending quite a lot of money on videos and CDs. I asked her why she had so much money and she said that her dad had increased her pocket money.

I've never had any reason to suspect Charlotte before, and I feel really guilty about it now but I think my boss is watching me. As it was me who recommended Charlotte, I'm worried about losing my job. How can I find out if Charlotte has been stealing or not, without actually accusing her?

Rebecca

Improve your writing

Telling a story

Writing this type of letter is like telling a story.

a Decide how you will locate your story in time and place.
Example
Recently I've been worried about ...
Two months ago I ...

b Decide who is telling the story. If you are telling the story personally, use the first person, *I*. If you are telling the story from someone else's viewpoint, use the third person, *a man/woman, she/he*, etc.

c Decide in which order or sequence you will place the events in your story. You can tell the story in the order that it happens or begin with the most dramatic part of the story.
Example
I work in a bakery on Saturdays. One day last week, our boss called all the staff into his office. Money was missing from the till and suddenly we were all under suspicion.

d When you tell a story you usually use past tenses. Progressive forms are useful for describing what was happening. Linking words like *while* make it clear that events are happening at the same time. The simple past tense tells the story and what has happened.

e Always think about who will be reading or listening to your story. What do they know already? What do they need to know? What style of language is it appropriate to use? Should it be formal or informal?

Vocabulary

Adjective + preposition

After some adjectives we can use a preposition (e.g. *of, about*).

Here are some common *adjective + preposition* combinations which express feelings towards people.

afraid of, angry with, annoyed with, fed up with, ashamed of, bored with, disappointed with/in, interested in, keen on, fond of, frustrated with, pleased with, suspicious of, tired of, worried about.

3 Sort the adjectives out into those which describe positive feelings and those which describe negative ones.

4 Use the adjective in brackets plus a preposition to write a new sentence describing how these people feel.

Example.
Rebecca is upset. She doesn't want to lose her job. (worried)
Rebecca is worried about losing her job.

1 The boss thinks Rebecca is guilty. (suspicious)
2 Rebecca is not pleased with Charlotte. (angry)
3 Rebecca has doubts about being Charlotte's friend. (ashamed)

Practice

5 Here is the same story from Charlotte's viewpoint. Put in the missing words.

works   because   ago   in   Although
At first   was enjoying   Then   but   should
with   so

My friend Rebecca (1) _____ in a bakery on Saturdays. Two months (2) _____ a vacancy came up. Rebecca asked me if I was interested (3) _____ the job. (4) _____ I didn't need the money I said yes (5) _____ I thought it would be a good experience. (6) _____, everything was fine. I (7) _____ the work and the responsibility and everyone was really friendly. (8) _____, some money went missing. Now I'm fed up (9) _____ the job. I know everyone suspects me (10) _____ nobody has talked to be me about it. Nobody talks to me and I want to leave. Dad has increased my pocket money (11) _____ I don't need the money. What (12) _____ I do? I don't want everyone to think that I left because I was guilty.

Writing

6 Arrange the pictures in order to tell a story.

7 Decide on something dramatic which happens after the last picture in the story.

8 Follow the *Improve your writing* guidelines and write the picture story. Write it in the form of a letter like the one about Charlotte and Rebecca. Start with the most dramatic part before describing the events leading up to it. Invent any details that you want to make the story more interesting. Be ready to read your story to the class.

Self check

9 Read your letter and decide if the sequence of events is clear and the tenses you have used are correct. Did you use any adjective+preposition phrases? If you didn't, add some to your story to describe how you felt about something or someone.

New Streetwise songbook

I'm eighteen

Lines form on my face and hands,
Lines form on the ups and downs,
Out in the middle, without any plans,
I'm a boy and I'm a (1) _____,
I'm eighteen and (2) _____,
Eighteen,
I just don't know what I want,
Eighteen,
I've got to get away,
I've got to get out of this place,
I'll go running in (3) _____.

I've got a baby's brain
And an old man's (4) _____,
Took eighteen years to get this far.
Don't always know what I'm talking about,
Feels like I'm living in the middle (5) _____,
Cos I'm eighteen.

I get confused every day,
Eighteen,
I just don't know they say,
Eighteen,
I got to get away.

Lines form on my face and my hands,
Lines form on the left and (6) _____,
I'm in the middle, in the middle of life,
I'm a boy and I'm a man,
I'm eighteen and (7) _____,
Yes, I like it,
Eighteen,
Yes I like it,
Eighteen, eighteen,
Oh, I like it, love it, like it, love it,
I'm eighteen and I like it.

1 Would you like to be eighteen? How would your life be different?

2 Look at the song and insert these missing phrases.

outer space
of doubt
man
I like it
I don't know what I want
right
heart

3 Listen and check your answers.

4 Does the singer like being eighteen? Why/Why not?

5 Discuss these questions in small groups.
Phrases in the song like 'Out in the middle without any plans' describe how he feels.

1 What do you think he means? Do you ever feel like this? When/Why?
2 What doesn't he like about being eighteen?
3 Which other phrases describe how he feels?

ISSUE **4**

NEW
Streetwise

The future

Are computers part of your everyday life? Why/Why not?

Interviews

How would you dress for an important interview?

The generation gap

What will you be like when you get old?

The future

Warm-up

1 Work in small groups and answer these questions.

1 What kind of things can you do on the Internet?
2 What do you think teenagers find most useful and enjoyable about the Internet?

Reading

2 You are going to read three young people's opinions of the Internet. Read the articles and decide who:

1 thinks the Internet will become less important.
2 thinks computers will change the way we shop.
3 thinks we will be able to speak to computers.
4 hasn't got a computer at home.
5 thinks the Internet is very slow.
6 thinks we do not really need computers.
7 believes computers will improve women's lives.
8 shops on the Internet.
9 thinks the Internet will improve their life.

Jake

I think the Internet is here to stay and will change all our lives for the better. For example, I think shopping as we know it will have disappeared by 2020 as it can be done electronically. Goods will be selected on screen and delivered to our door. I already buy books this way from an on-line bookshop and my mum orders her groceries on the net. I know that there are technical problems about the amount of information we can transmit but computer technology is increasing so fast that I am sure these problems will be solved. I think that in the future our computers will be part of the furniture. We'll talk to them, ask them questions, and have access to all the knowledge in the world.

Liam

I think people are attaching too much importance to computers and the Internet. Very few aspects of our daily life require computers. Computer technology is irrelevant to playing sport, cooking, driving, eating, speaking, having fun, and most of everyday life. You don't need a keyboard to play basketball. Have you tried surfing the net? It can take fifteen to thirty seconds for a single picture to appear. I think people will become bored with it and the Internet will just be another fad. I haven't got a computer and I'm not getting one either.

Caroline

I haven't got a computer at home but I hope that my parents will buy me one for my next birthday. I use a computer at College but with my own machine I'll be able to stay in touch with my friends and do a lot more research. I think the Internet will make women's lives easier. For example, my older sister is able to look after her baby and carry on working. She uses e-mail to stay in constant contact with her company. In a few years we'll be accessing the Internet from our TVs.

Vocabulary

3 Find words and expressions that mean:

1. connected to a system (o...- l...)
2. exploring the Internet (s... t... n...)
3. set of keys with words and numbers on you use to type (k...)
4. something that is popular for a very short time (f...)
5. remain in regular contact with (s... i... t...)
6. sending letters electronically (e-m...)

Talking point

4 Work in small groups and discuss the following:

- How do you think new computer technology will affect the quality of life?
- Which of these views is closest to your viewpoint?

1. I think the quality of life is being improved. Shopping, communicating and working by computer will save time, money, and energy and will particularly help people such as the disabled, elderly, and parents with young children.
2. I think it is damaging our physical and mental health. People will spend far too much time in front of a computer screen and not enough time playing sport, meeting, and communicating with people in the real world.

Improve your grammar

Future forms

a Look at these examples of different future forms in the text

1. *Shopping will have disappeared by 2020.*
2. *In a few years we'll be accessing the Internet from our TVs.*
3. *The technical problems will be solved.*

Which of these future forms do we use when:

1. the person doing the things is not known or not important?
2. something will have happened by a certain time?
3. something will be in progress at a certain time in the future?

b Complete the passage with *will* or *going to*.

Will and *going to* are both used for predictions. However, we use ____ for a prediction based on the present situation (e.g. what we can see is going to happen). *Look, the plane is on fire! It's* ____ *crash.* We use ____ for a prediction (what we think will happen). *One day people* ____ *live in space.*

Practice

5 Choose the best form. Give reasons for your answers.

1. He's got a new job at the university. **He's going to do/He'll do** research into the future.
2. New evidence suggests that people **will/are going to** holiday in space in the next few years.
3. The building will take ten years to finish. If they start soon they **will be finishing/will have finished** by the year 2000.

6 Complete these sentences using the future perfect.

Example
By/2020 shops/disappear.
By the year 2020 shops will have disappeared.

1. By/end/twenty-first century doctors find/cure for all diseases.
2. By/end/next century factory workers be/replaced by robots.
3. If we are not careful we destroy/world's/natural resources by 2010.
4. By/2010 I use/computers/twenty years.

7 Rewrite these sentences to keep the same meaning. Start with the words provided.

1. Someone will perfect anti-ageing drugs.
   Anti-ageing drugs _____ .
2. We will encourage children to stay at school longer.
   Children will _____ .
3. More people will work at home.
   More work _____ .
4. People will use more and more computers.
   More _____ .

Listening 📼

8 No-one likes referees but can computers and technology replace them? *New Streetwise* tries to find out. Listen to the report and decide if these statements are true or false.

1. Footballers can wear a monitor that tells us where they are.
2. There is a special camera which checks if the football is over the goal line.
3. A camera can tell if a penalty is deliberate.
4. Paul Dunkin thinks referees aren't needed.

Interviews

Reading 📼

1 Complete the text with these words:

dirty   chew   have   untidy   looks   nervousness   take   with   bag   wear

The smart way to get on

Doing well in an interview may be an important part of getting a place at university, a job, or a pass in an important exam. However, many young people fail to create the right impression because their appearance lets them down. New *Streetwise* looks at how to dress and behave on the big day.

Don't play with your hair, or (1) _____ your nails or fingers. It can be very off-putting and only highlights your (2) _____ .

Don't wear clothes that are scruffy and (3) _____ .

Don't (4) _____ your personal stereo – switched on or off!

Don't take a plastic (5) _____ – even for important documents like your CV or exam certificates – it always (6) _____ like you're carrying your dirty washing.

Don't wear (7) _____ shoes!

Do enter the interview room (8) _____ a bright and friendly smile, it counts for a lot.

Do dress smartly. Whether your clothes are old or new, (9) _____ them washed and pressed.

Do (10) _____ a shirt and tie if the interview demands it.

Glossary

scruffy: *untidy in appearance*

CV: *abbreviation for curriculum vitae – a brief written account of the main events of your life, details about yourself, your education, hobbies, jobs, etc.*

Listening 📼

Surviving an interview

2 Patrick Chan is having his first interview next week. *New Streetwise* took Patrick to see Sarah Brown, an expert on interview techniques. Listen and decide if these statements are true or false.

1 Pat is planning to wear his jacket.
2 His interview starts at eleven.
3 He is going by car.
4 Pat should try and talk to the other interviewees.
5 Pat should sit down as soon as he goes in the interview room.
6 He should always shake hands with the interviewers.
7 He should always look at the interviewers while he is talking.
8 He should ask questions.

In your opinion, which are the three most important pieces of advice?

Improve your grammar

Present progressive/simple present with a future meaning

a We use the present progressive for future events resulting from a present plan or arrangement.
Example *Dad is driving me.*

b We use the simple present for future events which are fixed by calendar or timetable, or because they are part of an unchangeable plan.
Example *The interview starts at eleven.*

c We use the simple present for future reference in clauses after *I hope, I assume*, etc.
Example *I hope you do well.*

d We use the simple present for the future after time expressions like *as soon as, before, after*.
Example *As soon as you are ready, someone will come and get you.*

Mark these sentences **a**, **b**, **c** or **d**.
1 My train leaves at ten.
2 I'm going to the cinema this evening.
3 We'll leave when he arrives.
4 Let's assume that he plays tomorrow.
5 He retires next week.
6 My brother's playing for United tomorrow.

Practice

3 Choose an appropriate present tense for each example.

1 My interview _____ (start) at ten twenty tomorrow.
2 Jane _____ (go) to London next week.
3 Tomorrow _____ (be) Tuesday the 10th of November.
4 How are you getting to my house? I _____ (come) by bus.
5 We _____ (meet) here at eight thirty. The bus _____ (leave) at nine. We _____ (plan) to visit the Royal palace first.

4 Pat is talking to a friend about his interview. Fill in the blanks. You may need more than one word in each space.

John	Hi Pat, when (1) _____ interview?
Pat	Next Friday.
John	(2) _____?
Pat	It starts at eleven.
John	How (3) _____?
Pat	My dad's driving me.
John	I (4) _____ next week.
Pat	Really! What is the interview for?
John	A scholarship to visit Japan.
Pat	What will you do when you get there?
John	It's a chance to see the country and learn some Japanese.
Pat	Well, I hope (5) _____. Let me know how you get on.
John	I'll get in touch as soon as (6) _____ the result of the interview.

Vocabulary

5 Match these verbs to the definitions.

put someone off   get worked up
turn someone down

1 refuse or reject someone
2 discourage
3 become angry or excited

6 Complete these sentences with the correct form of the verbs in exercise 5.

1 I went for the interview but they _____ because I had no experience.
2 Nothing _____ her _____ once she had made up her mind.
3 He _____ about the article because he did not agree with the writer's views.

Getting Streetwise! 📼

Fear and anxiety

7 Which of these adjectives best describes the way you normally feel before an important exam?

1 flustered = nervous and confused
2 cool, calm and collected = unemotional and unexcited
3 anxious = nervous and worried
4 confident = unworried, sure that you will do well
5 sick = ill in your stomach

8 Listen to what these teenagers feel about taking exams and complete the table.

	Worries about
Mike	
Alex	
Sandra	
Alan	

9 Listen again and see which of these expressions for expressing fear and anxiety were used by the panel.
What if ...
I'm absolutely dreading it ...
I'm terrified by ...
The thought of ... makes me sick
I just don't think I can ...
I'm afraid of ...

Which panel members do you identify with? Why?

The generation gap

Warm-up

1 Do you think that friction between young people and the older generation is inevitable? Why/Why not

Reading 📼

2 An old lady has sent a letter to *New Streetwise* about young people today. Read her letter and put in the missing expressions.

In conclusion,	They also say that
Their first argument	However,
On the other hand,	Their second argument
Furthermore,	but on the other hand

Is there hope for the future?

Many people of my generation say that there is no hope for the future because of the way that young people behave today.

(1) _____ is that when we were young we used to look after the older people in our community and help them. (2) _____ young people today don't care about anything or anyone. (3) _____ I think the reason why we looked after older people was that we had no choice. People had to live with their parents and grandparents because they had no money. Young people today earn more and have more freedom to live where they want. Despite this, I think that they're still interested in older people. For example, young people often offer to help me when I get on and off the bus with heavy shopping.

(4) _____ is that in our day we didn't expect to be given jobs – and that young people don't look for jobs, but just complain about unemployment. (5) _____ things were easier in the past and it was always easy to get a job if you had friends and contacts. I know that young people complain about unemployment but I think they have every reason to complain.

(6) _____ the older generation claim the youth of today seem to have no respect for their elders. They're always arguing with their parents these days. I think this is true, (7) _____ young people haven't changed since I was young. I loved my parents but we always argued about everything.

(8) _____ I think there is hope for the future. This generation, like generations before them, has new opportunities as well as old problems. If they learn from our mistakes the world will be a better place in future.

Talking point

3 Read these extracts before discussing the questions in small groups.

How *not* to talk to your mother
You are about to leave the house:
'Where are you going?'
'Out.'
'Out where?'
'Just out.'

You have just hung up the telephone:
'Who was that, dear?'
'Can't a person have some privacy once in a while!'

You have just returned from school:
'How did you do in the science test?'
'I don't want to talk about it.'

4 Are any of these conversations familiar? Would these conversations occur in your country? Why/Why not?

5 What are the reasons for conflict and friction between the generations in your country? What subjects and topics do you agree on? What subjects and topics do you usually disagree on? Is there one topic that causes the most problems?

Improve your writing

Writing a composition

a A composition is usually a follow-up to a class activity. It puts forward two or more views on a subject, for example, the case *for* and *against* something, or outlining the *advantages* and *disadvantages* of doing something. The main argument of the composition is usually given in the title.

b Begin by planning the content of your composition. Divide a sheet of paper into two columns. Note the main points *for* the argument in the left-hand column and the main points *against* in the right. Leave space after each point to add ideas and examples from your own experience.

c Use your list of points to write the first draft of your composition. Introduce the subject of your composition in the first paragraph.

d Then introduce the points from your left-hand column. These should agree with the argument of the essay. If the points are short, you can group two or three in one paragraph. If not, use a new paragraph for each new main point. Introduce each separate point clearly by using expressions like:
The first reason why ...
The second argument for thinking ...
In addition, ... Furthermore, ...

e Follow each point or group of points *for* the argument with points *against* the argument from the right-hand column. Make the contrast between sections clear, by using expressions like these to introduce the *against* points:
In contrast, .../However, .../On the other hand, ...

f In the final paragraph you should summarize and give your own view with reasons. Use expressions like:
To sum up, .../In conclusion ...
On balance, .../On the whole, ...

Practice

6 These are notes for a composition entitled *Young people today don't care. Discuss.* Divide the notes into two columns, one *for* and the other *against* the argument.

Young people today don't care about anything or anyone.
They take part in charity events.
They don't seem to want to do anything for themselves.
Very few young people are vandals.
The only thing young people worry about is fashion and the way they look.
In lots of places there are no facilities for the young.
Young people sit around moaning.
People who complain about the young often have no contact with them.
Young people would do more if they were allowed to.
The young vandalize property when they are bored.

Can you add any more points to either list?

7 Look at your two lists and decide on the order in which the points might appear if you were writing this composition.

Writing

8 Use the notes you have gathered to help you to write the composition entitled *Young people today don't care. Discuss.* Follow the *Improve your writing* guidelines and put the case *for* and *against*. Use examples from your own experience. In the concluding paragraph you should give your own opinion.

Self check

9 Check your work. Is the spelling, punctuation, and grammar correct? Are the arguments clear and logical? Re-draft your composition if necessary.

Grammar review

Issues 3 and 4

Present tenses

The options for talking about the past in English include the past simple, past progressive, *used to/would*, the past perfect, past perfect progressive, and present perfect.

Uses	Examples
1 Past simple: for a number of events which took place one after the other in the past.	*He came in, went to the window, and opened it.*
2 Past progressive: for an event which was in progress when another event happened.	*She was sleeping when the accident happened.*
3 Past progressive: to set the scene and provide the background for a story.	*The sun was shining brightly when Bob woke up.*
4 Past perfect: for an event which happened before another in the past.	*I went home because I had left my homework at home.*
5 Past perfect progressive: to talk about an action in progress up to the past time we are thinking about.	*I was very tired. I had been playing basketball all afternoon.*
6 Past perfect progressive: to show that an action was frequently repeated, before a past time we are thinking about.	*She had been biting her nails for years, but last month she gave up.*
7 Present perfect: for actions in the past that are not given a specific time.	*My brother has visited Australia.*

Future in the past

The future in the past can be expressed by *was going to*, *was about to*, and *was on the point of*.

Uses	Examples
1 To refer to events which were planned to take place and which did take place.	*When I got there she was about to leave, so I didn't really speak to her.*
2 To refer to events which were intended but which did not happen at the time because something interrupted or prevented them.	*I was about to go on holiday, but the airline went on strike.* *I was going to give her the money, but she didn't come.*

Notes
Was about to and *was on the point of* both carry the suggestion that the 'future in the past' event is very near. *It was 8.59 and the lesson was on the point of starting when he walked in.*
When we use *I was going to see him* or *I was about to see him* we need further information to know whether the meeting took place or was prevented from taking place.

Future forms

Uses	Examples
1 *be going to*: for an intention.	*I'm going to do my homework this evening.*
2 *be going to*: to indicate that something is probable.	*I think the plane is going to crash.*
3 *will/shall*: to make predictions.	*We will all live in cities in future.* *I think the sun will shine tomorrow.*
4 Future progressive: for an event that will be in progress at a certain time in the future.	*I'll be doing my exam this time next week.*
5 Future perfect: for an event which will be over not later than a certain time.	*Will you have finished by midnight?* *He will have gone home by then.*
6 Future passive: for the future where the person or agent doing the thing is not known or not important.	*It will be done.*

Note

Will (not *going to*) is used to express a sudden decision to do something in the future.
'Oh, the phone is ringing.' 'I'll answer it.'
I'm bored. What can I do? I know! I'll clean my bike.

Shall is the most commonly used:
1 to offer to do something.
   Shall I help you carry the shopping?

2 in suggestions.
   Shall we go and see a film tonight?

3 in requests for instructions.
   What shall I do next?

Future forms – present tenses

Uses	Examples
1 Present progressive: for future events resulting from a present plan, programme, or arrangement.	*I'm planning to wear a jacket.* *Dad's driving me.* *I'm thinking of studying medicine.*
2 Simple present: for the future in certain types of subordinate clause, especially adverbial time clauses and conditional clauses. Conjunctions which go with the present tense in this way are *after, before, once, until, when, as soon as, if, even if, unless, as long as.*	*When they are ready for you, someone will come and get you.* *As soon as he arrives, we'll start the lesson.* *She'll wait until you phone her.*
3 Simple present: '*that*' clauses following *hope assume, suppose,* etc. can also contain a verb in the present tense referring to the future.	*I hope you do well.* *Let's assume the team gets to the final.*
4 Simple present: for future events which are seen as absolutely certain, either because they are determined in advance by calendar or timetable, or because the are part of an unalterable plan.	*Tomorrow is a Saturday.* *The interview starts at eleven.* *He retires next month.*

Grammar practice

A ···

1 Complete the sentences with an appropriate form of the verb (past simple, past progressive or past perfect).

Example
He *wasn't playing* (not play) there. He *had left* (leave) before I *arrived* (arrive).

1 The concert _____ (begin) at nine last night.
2 She _____ (write) a letter when somebody _____ (come) in.
3 He _____ (do) five grammar exercises by lunch-time.
4 I _____ (see) him a month ago. He _____ (not go) to America yet.
5 He said that he _____ (not see) her for years.
6 It _____ (rain) at the time of the accident.

2 Choose the correct future form.

Example
I don't feel very well. ***I'm going to be/I'll be*** sick.

1 'How do you use this?' 'That's easy, ***I'll show/I'm going to show*** you.'
2 The train ***will have left/will be leaving*** by nine o'clock.
3 If he ***will go/goes***, I'll stay.
4 This time next week we ***will sit/will be sitting*** on the beach.
5 The radios ***will be made/will make*** in Japan.
6 'What are you doing tonight? '***I'm going to/I'll*** repair my bike.'

3 Join an idea in A with an idea from B. Make sentences using *was/were going to* and the verb in brackets.

A	B
1 He (study) medicine at university	but it was closed.
2 I (return) the book I borrowed	but we had pasta in the end.
3 I (go) to the concert	but he broke his hand.
4 We (fly) there	but they bought a computer instead.
5 He (play) in goal	but I couldn't get tickets.
6 They (buy) a typewriter	but he failed his exams.
7 We (have) pizza for lunch	but the airline went on strike.
8 They (visit) the museum	until she found out he was already married.
9 She (marry) him	but I left it at home.

B

1 Finish each of the sentences so that it means exactly the same as the sentence printed before it. Use verbs that express the idea of something happening in the future.

Example
I've decided to fly to Manchester next week.
I'm flying to Manchester next week.

1 I've decided to go to Italy for my holidays.
I'm _____ .
2 We will go on a city tour on arrival.
As soon as _____ .
3 The time of the next bus to London is 22.15.
The London bus _____ .
4 I've decided to start learning Spanish next month.
I'm _____ .
5 I predict a rise in prices next year.
In my opinion, _____ .
6 Someone will finish it.
It _____ .

2 Use *was going to* or *was about to* to write sentences for each situation.

a

b

c

d

e

f

Example
a *They were going to drive away when they discovered that their wheels were missing.*

3 Jane and Jim are talking about their weekend plans. Complete the conversation.

Jane Hi Jim! What (a) _____ ?
Jim I'm going to see my grandmother on Sunday Why?
Jane There (b) _____ a concert at the Apollo on Saturday.
Jim Who (c) _____ ?
Jane Robbie Williams.
Jim Have (d) _____ ?
Jane Yes, and I've got an extra ticket for you!
Jim That's fantastic. What time (e) _____ ?
Jane At eight. Let's meet my house at seven.
Jim Great! I (f) _____ then.
Jane I (g) _____ forward to seeing you.

4 Make the necessary changes and additions to write complete sentences.

Dear Carmen

1 I hope/be/well. I be/fine.
2 This time next week, I do/exams.
3 As soon as/exams finish/we go/holiday.
4 I really need/holiday by the time/exams be/over!
5 This year we go/the north of Spain.
6 I look/forward/it very, very much.
7 I write/you again when/get/there.
Yours,
Jim
8 PS I be/about to put this/the post when/get/your good luck card.
9 It be/lovely! Thanks for thinking/me.

C

1 Read this joke.

A naughty child was annoying all the passengers on the flight from London to New York. At last, one man couldn't stand it any more. 'Hey, kid,' he shouted. 'Why don't you go outside and play?'

Write your own joke in English.

2 Imagine that you are working in a travel agency. You have planned a week's dream holiday for a visitor from outer space. Use appropriate future tenses to tell your client about the holiday.

Example
On Monday you leave for the Caribbean. As soon as you arrive, you will be taken to a luxury hotel ...

ISSUE **5**

NEW
Streetwise

Visitors from space — Is this real?

Left-handers

What is special about these everyday things? Who are they for? Why?

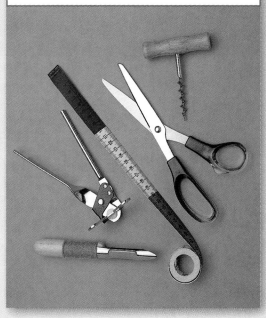

Films — What do you know about the story of Romeo and Juliet?

Visitors from space

Warm-up

1 Look at these statistics:
- 21% of UK adults believe in aliens
- 6% believe that people are sometimes kidnapped by aliens
- 1% believe that aliens have taken over people's minds

What do people in your country think about aliens? Do you believe in aliens? Why/Why not?

Listening 📼

Kidnapped by aliens
Travis Walton was working in the forest with five other men. His boss stopped the truck they were travelling in when they saw a flying saucer above the trees. Walton jumped out and ran towards it. The others panicked and drove off. When they returned, Walton and the flying saucer had gone. There was a huge search for him. Five days later Walton turned up with the story of his capture by an alien race. Walton's experience was made into a film and he has passed four lie detector tests.

2 Listen to extracts from Walton's statement and decide if these statements are true or false.

1 This wasn't the first saucer that Walton had seen.
2 He was afraid.
3 He ran away from the saucer.
4 The first people Walton saw looked human.
5 They had big eyes.
6 Walton saw a human in a helmet and uniform.
7 When he woke their saucer was gone.

Talking point

3 Work individually and prepare an alternative explanation of Walton's story. Share your ideas in a small group. Are any of your explanations more believable than Walton's story? Why/Why not? Do you believe Walton's story is possible? Why/Why not?

Reading 📼

4 Read the text 'Ancient space travellers' quickly and find:
- two arguments in favour of the idea that Earth was visited by ancient astronauts.
- two arguments against the idea.

5 Why are von Daniken's ideas so popular?

Ancient spac

The idea that aliens might have visited the Earth many years ago first became popular when *Chariots of the Gods?* was published in English. The author, Erich von Daniken, claims spaceships were observed in Mesopotamia thousands of years ago and the aliens revealed the secrets of metal making, agriculture, and written language to man. In support of his theories von Daniken points out that the mythologies of almost every culture include tales of winged animals and flying machines, and how some ancient drawings look similar to modern astronauts. He also argues that many ancient achievements and mysteries, from the building of the pyramids

Glossary

mythologies:
traditional fantasy stories to explain the past

ravellers

in Egypt, to the detailed maps of ancient sailors, were only possible with the help of these ancient space travellers.

Von Daniken's theories have been attacked by many scholars. For example, they argue that techniques used in the construction of the pyramids are now well known. His interpretation of early drawings has also been attacked. Would ancient space travellers really have looked like modern astronauts? However, lots of people have similar beliefs to von Daniken. After all, with so many unknown galaxies and stars, it is reasonable to assume that we are not alone. Isn't it?

Vocabulary

6 Match the definitions to the words as they are used in the text.

1	reveal	as evidence for
2	in support of	explanation of
3	interpretation of	varying between
4	ranging from	ideas
5	theories	effect
6	impact	make known

Practice

7 Change the sentences from active to passive.

1 Someone gave von Daniken information about spaceships.
Von Daniken _____ .
2 Von Daniken wrote *Chariots of the Gods?*
Chariots of the Gods? _____ .
3 The New York Times published his ideas.
His ideas _____ .
4 Someone had told people in Mesopotamia about metal making.
The people in Mesopotamia _____ .
5 Nobody believed me when I said that I had seen a UFO.
I _____ .
6 Someone helped them to build the pyramids.
They _____ .
7 They photographed him before his trip.
He _____ .

8 Expand the following to make sentences about Travis Walton's experience.

a Walton capture/aliens.
b He take/on board/spaceship.
c He put/on a table/alien creatures.
d He take/another room/a man in blue.
e Something/put/his face.
f He release/five/later.

Left-handers

Warm-up

1 Which hand do you normally use in these tasks?

1 Writing
2 Drawing
3 Throwing
4 Using scissors
5 Using a toothbrush
6 Using a knife (without a fork)
7 Using a spoon
8 When you strike a match, which hand do you hold the match with?
9 When you open a jar, which hand do you use to hold the lid?

Reading

2 Follow the instructions below Then read the text to find out what it says about you.
1 Draw the profile of a dog
2 Close your eyes.
3 Imagine that you're locked in a room, seated in a chair, with your hands tied behind you. In front of you is a telephone, your only means of rescue. Which foot do you use to pull the telephone closer?

Listening

3 Do you know anyone who is left-handed? What kind of problems can left-handed people face in everyday life?

4 Listen to a report on left-handed people and decide if these statements are true or false.

1 Some left-handed people have to learn to do things twice.
2 Left-handed children need special left-handed equipment.
3 It's easier for left-handed children to learn to write.
4 About half the population is left-handed.
5 Left-handers are usually less intelligent.
6 Left-handers are often better at tennis.

GET IT RIGHT! ●●●●●●●●●●●●●●●●●●●●●●●

Most people believe that we are either left- or right-handed. This is incorrect. You are probably more ambidextrous than you realize. For example, if you do a lot of things with your left hand, it is likely you can write quite well with your left hand.

Look at your drawing of a dog. Most right-handers draw the profile facing left and most left-handers draw it facing right.

Most people are right-footed as well as right-handed and right-eyed and they would reach out for the telephone with their right foot. However, if you're right-handed and you imagine reaching out with your left foot you might be a frustrated left-hander.

Glossary

ambidextrous:
able to use both hands equally well

Vocabulary

5 Complete the sentences with an appropriate word from this list.

reverse   forwards   anti-clockwise
sideways   opposite   backwards

1 Words like *level* and *noon* are palindromes. You can read them ____ as well as ____ .
2 tfel is an example of ____ writing.
3 You can buy left-hand clocks which run ____ , the natural direction for left-handers. Normal clocks run in the ____ direction.
4 A crab is an animal that doesn't walk forwards or backwards, but ____.

Improve your grammar

Passive structures for modals

Modal verbs like *must, can, could, may, might, will, would, shall, should,* and *ought to,* can all be used in the passive.
The form is modal + passive infinitive.
Examples
It must be done.
He ought to be invited.
Or modal + perfect passive infinitive.
Example
He might have been hurt.

Practice

6 Rewrite these sentences in the passive. Start with the word provided.

1 Someone must do it.
  It _____ .
2 Someone can help him.
  He _____ .
3 They might build a new swimming pool.
  A _____ .
4 Someone might give him a chance.
  He _____ .
5 They ought to have punished her.
  She _____ .
6 They should have helped her find a job.
  She _____ .
7 You must clean this room.
  This _____ .

7 What must be done to improve this classroom? Complete the sentences with *must* or *should* + the passive infinitive of the verbs in the box. Use each verb once.

paint   clean   repair   replace
lock   encourage

1 The broken windows _____ .
2 The walls _____ a light colour.
3 The graffitti on the desks _____ .
4 The map _____ with another one.
5 The classroom _____ at breaks and at lunchtime.
6 The students _____ to keep the new classroom clean.

Getting Streetwise! 📼

Expressing reservations

8 Listen to some young people discussing a Bill of Rights for left-handers.

1 Summarize each speaker's point of view. Which speaker do you agree with most?
2 Listen again. The speakers use expressions to express reservations. Tick the expressions you hear.
  The trouble is ...
  Well, the problem is that ...
  That may be true, but ...
  That may be so, but ...
  I'm still not sure ...
  I wouldn't disagree with that ...
  You've got a point ...
  I'm still not convinced that ...
  I not sure I'd agree that ...
  You may be right, but ...

Talking point

9 Work in small groups and answer these questions:
• Do you think left-handed people are discriminated against in any way?
• Many countries have a Bill of Rights that sets out the things that people are entitled to do. Do you think left-handers should have special rights? Why/Why not?

Films

Warm-up

1 Which of these is your favourite type of film? Match the type with the picture.

action film cartoon disaster film
horror film musical romantic comedy
science fiction thriller western

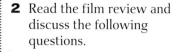

Shakespeare meets MTV –
A classic love story set in our time

Reading 📼

2 Read the film review and discuss the following questions.

1 What's the name of the film?
2 What type of film is it?
3 Which paragraph:
- tells us how the film opens
- tells us what the reviewer thinks of the acting
- tells us something about the director and the way he sees the film
- summarizes the reviewer's opinion
- tells us something about the story

Glossary

masked ball:
party with music and dancing where everyone wears a mask and costume

---

Romeo and Juliet is a modern version of the famous Shakespearean play. Although still a classic love story, *Romeo and Juliet* is a tale of young love in a violent modern world. The film is set around the exciting and fictional Verona Beach, which looks as glamorous as Miami, America. The film opens and closes dramatically with a news broadcast which tells us what is happening and introduces the main characters.

Romeo (Leonardo DiCaprio) and Juliet (Claire Danes) are the young lovers, full of passion and romance.

The Montague family and the Capulet family hate each other. When Romeo Montague, an uninvited guest at the Capulets' masked ball, meets and falls in love with Juliet Capulet, neither of them knows that they are family enemies and that their love can only lead them to a tragic end.

There's a great pop soundtrack, glamorous costumes and good-looking actors, but the film still uses Shakespeare's original dialogue. In addition, some of the most important lines are flashed onto the screen, which makes Shakespeare's language even more memorable and easy to understand.

Romeo and Juliet is a wonderful film. I think it has helped young people to enjoy this Shakespeare love story in a new way. The film's message of passionate young love is still just as relevant today. It was really romantic and beautiful and I cried at the film's sad ending. I give it 10 out of 10.

Improve your writing

Writing a film review

a Start by describing what kind of film you are writing about and where it is set.
You can do this directly, by stating the facts.

Example
The Beach is set on a beach in Thailand.
It is a thriller ...

Or indirectly, by briefly describing the beginning.

Example
A young backpacker arrives on a beautiful beach ...

Use past tenses to talk about facts about how the film was made, etc.

Example
The film was made on location in Thailand.

b Include the main points of the story and introduce the main characters. You can include the name of the actor in brackets. Make sure you don't tell the whole story and give too much irrelevant information.

Example
When Richard (Leonardo DiCaprio) arrives he meets ...

c Say what you liked or didn't like about the film. Use adjectives to describe what you thought.

Example
The film is amusing in places but also very exciting.

Try to talk about good and bad parts. Use linking words like *although*, *however*, and *but* to convey contrasting ideas.

Example
Although the story is quite exciting it needed a bit more action at times.

Use words like *and*, and *in addition* to join related ideas.

Example
The setting was really beautiful and in addition so were the actors!

d End with a short summary giving your overall opinion.

Example
If you like Leonardo DiCaprio go and see this film.
I can really recommend it. It is worth seeing.

Vocabulary

3 Match the words in italics to the definitions.

The film has *stunning* costumes and scenery.
This is a *light-hearted* romantic comedy.
The cartoon is full of *hilarious* characters.
The scene where Juliet wakes up to find Romeo dead is truly *moving*.
The special effects make the film *memorable*.
The plot, especially the part when the boy becomes a politician, is *ridiculous*.
The part when the aliens appear is *terrifying*.

1 causing strong feelings
2 very silly or foolish
3 easy to remember because it is special
4 very funny
5 very frightening
6 funny; amusing
7 very attractive or impressive

Practice

4 Use *although* to join these sentences.

1 DiCaprio is handsome. He isn't a great actor.
2 The film is very long. It holds your attention.
3 The film was made in the studio. It looks real.
4 The actress is English. She plays an American.

5 Complete the sentences with *however*, *although*, and *in addition*.

1 The plot is silly. ___ , I really enjoyed it.
2 ____ the film is almost three hours long, it wasn't boring.
3 Leonardo Di Caprio was great in Titanic. ____ he gave a superb performance in *The Beach*.
4 Titanic fails as a love story. ____ , it is a great disaster film.
5 This is the Director's first film. ____ , it's the first time he has worked in Hollywood.
6 ____ the special effects are stunning, the acting is terrible.

Writing

6 Follow the *Improve your writing* guidelines and write a review of a recent film for a teenage magazine. If possible, illustrate it.

Self check

7 Read a review and mark it from 1–5 for each of these areas.

- Does the review tell you enough?
- It is clearly organization in distinct paragraphs?
- Does the reviewer use linking words to join ideas and phrases?

New Streetwise songbook

Teenager in love

1 Each time we have a quarrel
2 'Cause I am so afraid
3 Each night I ask the stars up above,
4 One day I feel so happy,
5 I guess I'll learn to take
6 Each night I ask the stars up above,
7 I cried a tear
8 I'll be a lonely one
9 Well if you want to make me cry
10 If you should say we're through,

a why must I be a teenager in love?
b next day I feel so sad.
c I'll still go on loving you.
d that we will have to part.
e it almost breaks my heart,
f that won't be so hard to do.
g the good with the bad.
h for nobody but you.
i why must I be a teenager in love?
j if you should say goodbye

1 Do you think it is difficult to be a teenager in love? Why? Discuss how these things can affect a relationship. Which is the biggest problem? Why?

• school
• parents
• money
• friends

2 Look at the song. Match the two halves of each line. Use the rhyme in the second half of each line to help you.

3 Listen and check your answers.

4 What is the singer afraid of? Why?

5 Look at this quote from an article about teenage weddings and discuss these questions in small groups.

> Young love isn't true love and shouldn't be encouraged.
> Real love comes with maturity and experience.

1 Do you agree? Why/Why not?
2 What is the easiest age to be in love? Why?
3 Do you think young love doesn't last? Why/Why not?
4 At what age do you thing you can truly be in love?

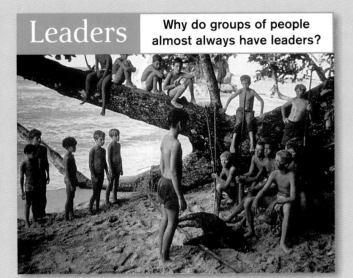

Leaders

Why do groups of people almost always have leaders?

Imitators

Who, if anyone, would you like to imitate? Why?

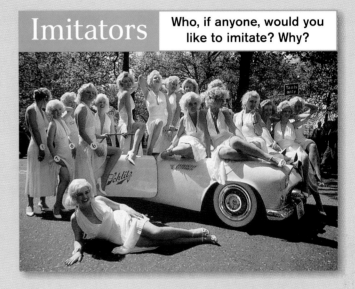

Teenage problems

Why do people write to magazines about their problems? Would you?

ask **anything**

If you've got a problem you need h
send it to Sarah and Wendy at **Su,**
17 Berners Street, London W1P 3L

School strain is too much

I've always done really well at school and, until a few months ago, I was top of my class. But last year I became ill and had to miss two terms of lessons. I got behind with my work and now I've slipped to the bottom of the class.

My teachers say I should be able to catch up if I work hard, but I can't seem to do it. Everything used to come easily to me, but I'm finding it hard to come to terms with my illness as well as getting on with my work. I'm pretending everything's OK but it's not. Can you help me?

Boyzone fan, Torbay

Wendy says I'm sorry you're having such a difficult time, but the only way you're going to stop this situation getting worse is by admitting that you're struggling.

You've been through a traumatic experience and if you tell a teacher how you feel, I'm sure they'll understand and try to ease your workload until you feel you can manage better. Take some time out to relax and get back to enjoying life, too.

I also think you should seek counselling to help you come to terms with how this illness has affected you. Youth Access (see help box) can put you in touch with a counsellor.

"You've been through a traumatic experience"

Dear Vic

I've
unf

I've bee
boyfrie
I love hi
other ni
without
getting
rememl
my frier
off with
stop thi
I feel I
I'm also
to lose i
think I s
happen

Wendy
hard wa
people tr
and hope
same mi
whether
up to yo
be a lot
what he
than fro
how so
strongly

Hop
chanc
relatio
was b

**DON'T WANT MY
LAD TO JOIN THE
ARMY**

I really fancy the lad in the chip shop...

I really like this lad who works in the chip shop near us. I have always been shy around lads but I come out of my shell when I get to know them. I don't think I am good-looking but my best friend says I am because I have long dark brown/blonde hair.

Because I'm so shy I decided to write a letter to give to him, but I was too embarrassed to hand it over. Whenever go in he always says hello and starts chatting me up as though he's known me for a long time. He's even said, "Evening sweetheart", and one of the women who works with him looked at me as if to say, 'You're in there'.

My problem is I don't think anybody would go out with me. I have problems with my stomach and I've got somethin wrong with my back, too. There are other things I'm not happy about:
1. I don't wear shoes, always trainers.
2. Because I have long hair, I never ha it up in a pony tail.
3. I mainly wear shellsuits, Kappa stuf or army trousers.
4. I never wear make-up.
5. If we went on a date I wouldn't kno where to go, or what to talk about.
6. I'm scared he's going to laugh at the pop groups I like.

A PROBLEM SHARED...

I
M

his c
It's
com
won
I'll r

It'
grow
work
of th
close
start

Y
shar
of di
thos
siste
squa
that
make
E-ma
happ

N
fears
givin
char

My Mum's Miserable

I've got a big problem. My mum is really unhappy all the time. I try to talk to her but she shuts me out. Once she told me she was upset because my brother spends his time smoking and drinking with

S

Leaders

Warm-up

1 Make a list of six of the written or unwritten rules you follow in everyday life.

Example
You shouldn't talk when other people are talking.

Share your list with the class and see if any of the rules appeared in more than one list.

Reading 📼

Lord of the Flies by William Golding is a classic of English literature. A plane crash leaves a group of boys on a tropical island without any adults. In this extract from the beginning of the book, the boys decide what to do next.

2 Read the extract and answer these questions.

1 Which of the boys seems to be the leader?
2 Which of the boys wants to be a 'hunter'?
3 What rule did they decide on for the group?
4 Why did the boys get excited when Jack told them they would need lots more rules?'

Follow the leader

Ralph cleared his throat, 'Well then.'
All at once he found he could talk fluently and explain what he had to say. He passed a hand through his hair and spoke.
'We're on an island. We've been on the mountain-top and seen water all round. We saw no houses, no smoke, no footprints, no boats, no people.'
Jack broke in.
'All the same you need an army – for hunting.'
'There aren't any grown-ups. We shall have to look after ourselves.'
The meeting hummed and was silent.
'And another thing. We can't have everybody talking at once. We'll have to have "Hands up" like at school.'
He held the conch before his face and glanced round the mouth.
'Then I'll give him the conch.'
'Conch?'
'That's what this shell's called. I'll give the conch to the next person to speak. He can hold it when he's speaking.'
'But –'
'Look –'
'And he won't be interrupted. Except by me.'
Jack was on his feet.
'We'll have rules!' he cried excitedly. 'Lots of rules. Then when anyone breaks 'em –'
'Whee-oh!'
'Wacco!'
'Bong!'
'Doink!'

Vocabulary

3 Find words or phrases in the text that mean:

1 smoothly without any hesitation or mistakes
2 interrupted
3 finding and killing animals for food

Listening 📼

4 What do you think will happen to the group of boys? Choose a or b in each case. Give reasons for your answers.

1 They make rules …
  a and survive happily as a group until they are rescued.
  b but there is conflict between different groups of boys.
2 Some of the boys become hunters. The hunters …
  a only kill for food.
  b begin to kill for pleasure.
3 The boys …
  a respect each other.
  b begin to persecute each other.
4 At the end …
  a all the boys are rescued.
  b some of the boys are rescued.
  c none of the boys are rescued.

Now listen and check your answers. How accurate were your predictions? Why do you think groups in unusual situations lose control of themselves so easily?

....
Glossary

persecute: to treat badly
....

Talking point

5 Work in small groups and discuss these questions.

1 If you were in the same situation as the boys which three of these rules would you choose? Why?

• The group will have a leader and everyone has to obey that leader.
• Everyone in the group must love the other members of the group.
• Everyone must meet to discuss problems once a week.
• Everyone in the group will vote to decide on what to do next.
• Everyone in the group is allowed to do what they want.
• Everyone has to do a job that is good for the group.
• Anybody who bullies another member will be punished.

2 What other rules could you suggest to help your group live in peace?

Improve your grammar

Conditionals with *if* and *unless*

a Rewrite this sentence starting with *if*.
Unless you have the conch, you can't speak.
What is the meaning of *unless*?

b What would you do if you were living on the island?
Why do we use *would* in the question rather than *will*?

Practice

6 Complete these sentences with *if* or *unless*.

1 They won't survive ____ they have water.
2 They will fight ____ they don't have rules.
3 You can't speak ____ you don't have the conch.
4 He's short-sighted. He can't see things in the distance ____ he wears glasses.

7 Complete each sentence so that it means the same as the sentence printed before it.

1 She won't win the election, if we don't help.
  Unless _____ .
2 Unless we change the rules, she'll leave.
  If _____ .
3 We couldn't live there without water.
  Unless _____ .
4 I wouldn't help her if she didn't change.
  Unless _____ .

8 Rewrite these, starting with the word in brackets and keeping the same meaning.

1 Finish your homework. You can't watch the match until you do! (Unless …)
2 You can go out. But make sure you are back by eleven. (If …)
3 I wouldn't go without a ticket. (Unless …)
4 Work hard, or you won't get on in life. (If …)

Pronunciation 📼

Contrastive stress

9 Listen and mark the main stress in B's answers.

1 **A** She'll leave if we change the rules.
  B No, she'll leave unless we change them.
2 **A** He'll leave unless we change the rules.
  B No, she'll leave unless we change them.
3 **A** She'll stay if we don't change the rules.
  B No, she'll leave if we don't change them.

Why is a different word stressed in each one?

Listen again and repeat. Then practise with a partner.

Imitators

1 Have you ever tried to look like someone else? What do you feel about people who try to look like someone famous? How would you feel if someone wanted to imitate you?

Reading 📼

2 Read the text and complete it with these expressions.
- I just think, 'What great taste we've both got.'
- I suppose there's always going to be a bit of rivalry between friends but it's great to be the first person to get something.
- But if he started wanting everything that I've got, I know it would drive me crazy.
- She has no ideas of her own – it's pathetic!
- but would it feel like a compliment to you?

Is imitation really so flattering?

To be called a copy-cat in the school playground is considered an insult. But should you feel pleased when people you know well say how much they like your new jeans and then buy exactly the same style? Some people might find this flattering, (1) _____

I think we all imitate our friends a bit, says Sarah, 18. 'If I've had a good idea about what to do at the weekend or found a great new shampoo I'm only too happy to share these things. If I turn up at a party and find my friend dressed exactly like me, I actually feel more confident. (2) _____ '

There's nothing more irritating, says Megan, 17. 'I have a friend who always copies my clothes and haircuts. I wish she wouldn't. (3) _____ '

I suppose I should feel flattered, but actually it makes me cross, says Jack, 18. 'Recently I saved up for this new lightweight mountain bike and was feeling really pleased with myself — until my friend rushed out and bought exactly the same model.(4) _____ '

It depends on what they're copying, says Phil, 16. 'I was quite pleased when my best friend decided to do Spanish evening classes too because I like having someone to do my homework with. (5) _____ '

Glossary

It's pathetic:
expression used to show disapproval (informal)

3 Place Sarah, Megan, Jack, and Phil somewhere on this scale. Where would you place yourself? Why?

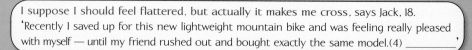

Most in favour of being imitated   Least in favour of being imitated

Vocabulary

4 Find words and phrases in the text that mean:

1 someone who copies your behaviour, etc. (c...)
2 praise, often about the way you look (c...)
3 annoying (i...)
4 rather angry (c...)
5 active competition between people (r...)
6 makes me mad/very angry (d... m... c...)

5 Match the sentences to the words below.

1 If I don't **get through** this time, I'll have to do my exams again.
2 I wish I could **get out of** doing the dishes.
3 I wish I could **keep up with** the others. They walk so fast.
4 If only we could **do away with** homework, there would be more time for having fun!

abolish   pass   go at the same speed as
avoid (a responsibility or duty)

Improve your grammar

Wish ... would

a *Wish ... would* expresses a wish for a change in how someone else behaves.
Examples
I wish you would be more polite.
I wish she wouldn't copy my hairstyle.

b We use the same pattern to express a wish for someone to do something, or for something to happen.
Examples
I wish you would tell me the news.
I wish that dog would stop barking.

Wish + simple past tense

c *Wish* and *If only* with a simple past verb express a wish for the present situation to be different.
Example
I wish I lived in New York. (but I don't)
If only I had a CD player. (but I haven't)

d With the verb *be* we can use *was* or *were* for 1st and 3rd person forms. *Were* is more formal than *was*.
Examples
I wish I was David Beckham. (but I'm not)
If only I were taller. (I'm not.)
My room is very small. I wish it was bigger.
(Not ~~I wish my room would be bigger.~~)

Practice

6 Imagine that you are the people in these situations and make sentences with *I wish +* simple past or *I wish + would* for each of these situations.

1 Alan is miserable because everyone else has new trainers but he hasn't.
2 Alison read in the papers that they are still killing elephants. She wants them to stop.
3 Alex's brother never does his homework.
4 Rosa wants a job in as a tour guide but she can't speak English.
5 Joe is a painter but he wants to be a famous singer.
6 Max is a farmer. The weather is hot and dry and it hasn't rained in months.
7 Rupert wants to go to sleep but there are noisy children playing outside.
8 Helena smokes thirty cigarettes a day. She wants to give up.

7 Complete these sentences.

1 I wish I had ...
2 I wish I were ...
3 If only I could ...
4 I wish it were Sunday because ...
5 I wish my best friend would ...
6 If only people wouldn't ...

Getting Streetwise! 📼

Surprise and disbelief

8 The following expressions can all be used to express surprise and disbelief. Do you have equivalent expressions in your language? What intonation would you use?

No!   Never!   You're joking.
You're pulling my leg.   That's amazing.
I don't believe it.
Really?   Wow!

Listen and repeat with appropriate intonation.

Complete these extracts with a suitable expression from the list above.

Extract 1
A There is this guy who claims he saw Elvis in a petrol station.
B _____ .
A No I'm not. He really claims to have seen him.
B Well, _____ .
A Neither do I.

Extract 2
A Mike's just returned the CD he borrowed last year.
B _____ .
A He has!
B Well, that's incredible. I never thought I would see it again.

9 In pairs, write and perform your own mini-dialogue using these expressions.

Teenage problems

Warm-up 📼

1 These extracts from letters to *New Streetwise* are all from people who suffer badly from the same problem. Read the extracts before discussing the questions in small groups.

1 What problem are they suffering from?
2 What are the symptoms and how does it affect people?
3 What advice would you give someone who suffers from this?

When I see an item of clothing in a shop, I am afraid to go in and buy it. Every time I try to go into a shop I get embarrassed when the shop assistant speaks to me. I always think they're thinking 'Nothing in this shop would ever suit her.'
Alex

I know some people who can't talk because of shyness. My problem is the complete opposite - I can't stop talking! You see, if a member of the opposite sex comes to talk to me, instead of going quiet I'm so nervous that I chat like mad.
John

I have no self-confidence and try not to talk to people as I am sure they wouldn't want to talk to me. I have started to think that this is because I am the world's most boring person.
Joanna

Vocabulary

2 What is the difference between:
advice and *advise*?
embarrassed and *embarrassing*?

3 Choose the correct form.

1 I was so *embarrassed/embarrassing* that I went red.
2 I find situations like this very *frightened/frightening*.
3 Pop music is so *bored/boring*.
4 His problem is very *worried/worrying*.
5 Exams are *terrified/terrifying*.
6 Were you *disappointed/disappointing* by what you saw?
7 The news was *depressed/depressing*.
8 My friends have been very *encouraged/encouraging* about my trip.

4 Complete the table.

	Adjective	Abstract noun
shy		shyness
friendly		
tired		
happy		
weak		

Now complete these sentences with nouns or adjectives from the table.

1 Money did not bring him ____ .
2 I hadn't eaten for days. I was ____ from hunger.
3 ____ is not one of his qualities. He is always arguing with people.
4 Do you suffer from ____ after a long day at school?
5 He is so ____ that he goes red when someone enters a room.

Improve your writing

Giving advice in writing

a Decide on your audience. What do they already know about the topic? Try to have an informal, friendly style.

b Make sure that any advice you give is clear by starting with a sentence outlining the problem.
Example
As your main problem is talking to people you don't know, why don't you try ...

c Use appropriate expressions like these to introduce your advice (those with asterisks are more formal than the others).
Advising someone to do something
If I were you I would ...
*It would be a good idea if ... ***
Unless you do this, you won't ...
You ought to ...
*Perhaps you should ... ***
Advising against something
Whatever you do, don't ...
Never listen ...
*It's best not to ... ***
You shouldn't ...

Practice

5 This is a reply to Joanna's letter. Put the sentences in the best order.

1 They might even think you don't like them.

2 It helps to put them at their ease.

3 If I were you I would start smiling and talking to people.

4 It is by no means true that you are the most boring person in the world.

5 That is your defence against having to meet new people.

6 As soon as you do this they will respond.

7 If necessary tell people you are shy.

8 Unless you do this people will think you are cold.

9 If you follow this advice, you will soon discover that other people can be boring too.

10 Yours,

11 Dear Joanna,

6 Complete this reply to Alex's letter with these words.

support   makes   problem   shops
into   were   If   and   the   will
could   come   It

Dear Alex,

I have the same (1) _____ , I don't like going into (2) _____ either.

If I (3) _____ you, I would start by going (4) _____ shops and just looking around. (5) _____ doesn't matter if you (6) _____ out without buying anything. (7) _____ you are comfortable with being in (8) _____ shop you can ask questions (9) _____ hold clothes up to you body. Finally, you (10) _____ be able to try things on. Perhaps you (11) _____ take a friend as well. This (12) _____ shopping easier and you will have moral (13) _____ .

Writing

7 Imagine that you are a victim of bullying. Follow the *Improve your writing* guidelines and write a letter in which you ask *New Streetwise* for advice.

Exchange letters with someone else. Write a reply to their letter in which you give advice on how to deal with their problem.

Self check

8 Read the reply to your letter. Did the writer follow the *Improve your writing* guidelines? Did they include any of the suggested expressions? Check their spelling and punctuation. What did you think of their advice?

Grammar review

Issues 5 and 6

Passive

Form

The appropriate tense of be (e.g. *is, was, is being, have been*, etc.) + past participle (*made, seen, written*, etc.)

It	is	
	has been	
	was being	cleaned.
	had been	
	will be	
	is going to be	

Uses

1 When we do not know who or what does something.

2 When the 'doer' of the action is not important. This is quite common in scientific writing.

3 The use of *by* + the passive gives special emphasis to the 'doer'.

Examples

Two men have been killed in a bomb attack in Northern Ireland today. My car was stolen.

In the first experiment, subjects were given a small amount of tea.

This cake was made by my youngest brother. The Walkman was invented by a Japanese company.

Notes

The passive is used in both spoken and written English, but it is probably more common in writing. It is often found in textbooks and reports as well as notices and announcements.
The substance is weighed twice in order to ...
Candidates are required to be present ten minutes before the exam starts.
Lunch will be served at 1 p.m.

The passive is also common in news reports.
A bomb exploded in the city centre yesterday, but luckily nobody was injured.
Twenty men were arrested after the football match.

Passive structures for modals

Form

modal + passive infinitive, e.g. *It can't be done.*
modal + perfect passive infinitive, e.g. *It can't have been done.*

Uses
Can, could, must, may, might, will, would, shall, should, ought to can all be used in the passive.

Examples
This car can be driven.
He must have been here.
He should be stopped.
He might have been hurt.

Passive conditional

Form

if + simple past + *would* + infinitive

Uses

1 To talk about unreal or hypothetical present or future situations.

2 To talk about present or future situations that are not likely.

Examples

What would you do if you went to live on the island?

If I won a car, I would be thrilled.

Note

The choice between the first conditional (*if* + simple present + *will* + infinitive) and the second conditional depends on our view as to how likely or possible something is. We use the first conditional if we think something is likely, and the second conditional if we think it is not, so the second conditional is used for hypothetical situations. Compare:
If I get Grade A in my English exam, I will be very pleased. (= It is possible that I will get Grade A).
If I got Grade A in my English exam, I would be very pleased. (= I think it is unlikely that I will get Grade A.)

Unless

Unless + positive = *if* + negative.
Unless usually means the same as *if* + negative. Compare:
If you don't have the conch, you can't speak.
Unless you have the conch, you can't speak.
But note that *unless* means 'except on the condition that' and it therefore cannot replace *if* in sentences like:
I'll be surprised if he doesn't come.

Wish ... would

Form

wish + object + *would* + infinitive

Uses	Examples
1 To express a wish for a change in how someone behaves.	*I wish she wouldn't copy my hairstyle.* *I wish you would be more polite.*
2 To express a wish for someone to do something, or for something to happen.	*I wish you would tell me what the problem is.* *I wish that dog would stop barking.*

Note

If we want to express a wish for a change in our own behaviour, we use *I wish I could* + infinitive and not *I wish I would ...*
I wish I could stop smoking.

Wish + simple past

Form

wish and *if only* + simple past

Uses	Examples
To express a wish for the present situation to be different. These wishes are generally impossible and therefore hypothetical.	*I wish I were Elvis.* *My room is very small. I wish it was bigger.* *If only I was taller, I could play in the basketball team.*

Notes

We can use *were* for first and second person forms.
Were is more formal than *was*.
I wish I were/was rich.
Liz wishes she were/was on holiday.
We cannot use *would* in these types of wishes.
I wish my room was bigger. (**Not** ~~I wish my room would be bigger.~~)
We can use *could* in these types of wishes.
I wish I could play the guitar, but I can't.

Grammar practice

A ··

1 Complete these sentences with an appropriate passive form of the verb in brackets.

Example
Romeo and Juliet *was written* (write) by William Shakespeare.

1 I _____ (give) a watch for my last birthday.
2 The stadium _____ (build) by this time next year.
3 Oranges _____ (grow) in California.
4 He told me his bike _____ (steal) during the night.
5 I hope that a homework machine _____ (invent) soon.
6 A lot of money _____ (spend) on education in recent years.
7 These sweets _____ (make) in our town for centuries.
8 We _____ (not tell) the answers to the last test.

2 Complete the sentences using an appropriate form of the verbs in brackets: simple present, simple past, *will, won't, would(n't)*.

Example
I'll tell (tell) your mother unless you stop.

1 I _____ (help) if I could.
2 I'll lend Peter the money if he _____ (need) it.
3 Provided they had plenty to eat, they _____ (be) happy.
4 Would you marry the prince if he _____ (ask) you.
5 Unless Chris improves, she _____ (fail) the exam.
6 If I _____ (be) you, I would go.

3 What would you say? Use *I wish ... would/wouldn't* to write an appropriate sentence for each situation.

Example
Your brother plays very loud music while you are doing your homework.
I wish you wouldn't play loud music while I'm doing my homework.

1 You are on a long walk. Your sister is walking very slowly.
2 A friend has got you into trouble by talking to you in class again.
3 One of the students in your class always speaks softly when he answers a question and you can't hear the answer.
4 Your brother always borrows your favourite jacket when you want to wear it.

5 You are the only member of your family who remembers to feed your pet cat.
6 The person who shares your bedroom never tidies it and you always have to do it.
7 You really like hamburgers, but your mother never cooks them.

B ··

1 Rewrite these sentences in the passive. Start with the word provided.

Example
Someone can tell him the good news.
He can be told the good news.

1 You must help her.
  She _____ .
2 Someone might have told him.
  He _____ .
3 Could someone invite him?
  Could _____ .
4 They ought to have helped people who were in trouble.
  People _____ .
5 I hope someone can invent a cure for cancer soon.
  I hope a _____ .
6 Someone ought to prevent him from doing this.
  He _____ .

2 The *New Streetwise* panel had a discussion about the problems of tall people. Use the passive to report their opinions.

Example
'People shouldn't laugh at them.'
They shouldn't be laughed at.

1 'Someone should make longer beds.'
2 'We could open special clubs for tall people.'
3 'We needn't treat them specially.'
4 'We ought to give them special cars.'
5 'We should also help short people.'
6 'We can't give special treatment to all the minorities.'

3 Finish each of the sentences so that it means the same as the sentences printed before it.

1 Unless Sarah leaves soon she will miss her bus.
  If _____ .
2 The match will be cancelled if the weather is bad.
  Unless _____ .
3 I won't lend him the money unless he needs it.
  If _____ .
4 I won't see him if he doesn't apologize.
  I refuse _____ unless _____ .
5 Without our goalkeeper, we would lose more matches.
  If _____ .
6 Unless anyone has questions, the lesson is over.
  If _____ .

4 Add an appropriate end to each sentence.

Example
I am very shy. I wish *I were more confident.*

1 I can't ride a horse. If only _____ .
2 The weather is very hot! I wish _____ .
3 We don't have tickets for the concert. If only _____ .
4 Life is boring! I wish _____ .
5 I can't play basketball. If only _____ .
6 I don't like my hair. I wish _____ .
7 Maria doesn't get good marks. She wishes _____ .

5 Complete each sentence so that it means the same as the one before it.

Example
I want to be able to speak English fluently.
I wish I spoke English fluently.

1 I would like to help you but I can't.
  I wish _____ .
2 He would like to be rich, but he's poor.
  He wishes _____ .
3 He doesn't want you to copy his homework.
  He wishes you _____ .
4 I would like to be at the beach right now and not in this exam.
  I wish _____ .
5 I want them to be more helpful.
  If only _____ .

C ··

1 Imagine that you are part of a group living on a desert island. Use the passive form of modals such as *can, should, must, needs to be*, etc., to write down ten 'rights' or 'rules' which are essential if you are to live together peacefully.

Example
Each person must be given enough food.

2 Write a paragraph describing some of the things you would or wouldn't do if you went to live on your dream island.

3 Do your relatives do anything that really annoys you? Use *I wish + would, could, were,* etc. to list six of your major complaints.

Example
I wish my aunt wouldn't always talk about what I was like when I was a baby.

Weddings

How do people normally meet the person they are going to marry?

The way we are

Do we change our personality when we change our clothes?

Girls in school

What do people in your country think of mixed schools?

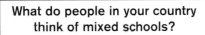

Weddings

Warm-up

1 Work in small groups and discuss what makes a really romantic wedding.

Reading 📼

2 Read the text quickly and decide if these statements are true or false.

1 The couple got married in a church.
2 They had never met before the ceremony.
3 The couple were there because they had won a competition.
4 They only had to answer some questions to win.
5 Their parents were very happy.
6 Many organizations did not approve of this wedding.
7 One of their prizes was a free wedding.
8 The writer expects the wedding to last.

Glossary

ivory: *colour of an elephant's tusk*

marriage guidance service: *an organization that helps people with marriage problems*

wedding breakfast: *the meal following the wedding celebration*

Two strangers and a wedding

The wedding took place in a Birmingham hotel. The bride and her father arrived in a new black American convertible sports car. Her father looked tense and uncomfortable in front of the cameras. The bride wore a stunning full-length ivory silk wedding dress. She smiled nervously at the waiting photographers and went to a room on the first floor where she met her future husband for the very first time.

Carla Germaine and Greg Cordell were the winners of a radio station's competition. The aim of the competition was to find two strangers prepared to marry without having met each other. Miss Germaine, 23, is a model. Mr Cordell, 27, is a TV salesman. They were among the two hundred entrants in a bizarre 'experiment' organized by BMRB radio in Birmingham, England. Greg and Carla were among eight finalists who were interviewed live on radio. They took a lie detector test and the station also spoke to their friends and family about their personalities The competition judges included an astrologer who looked at the couple's horoscope and declared that they were suited.

The couple celebrated their wedding with a wedding breakfast and a party for 100 guests in the evening, but not everyone shared their joy. Miss Germaine's mother looked anxious throughout the wedding and Mr Cordell's parents are reported to be less than delighted.

Organizations, including the marriage guidance service Relate, have condemned the marriage. As one person put it, 'We have enough problems getting young people to take marriage seriously without this. Marriage should always be about love.'

The couple are now on a Caribbean honeymoon accompanied by journalists and a film crew. Their other prizes include a year's free use of a luxury apartment in the centre of Birmingham, and a car. But will it last?

Vocabulary

3 Find words and phrases in the text that mean:

1 worried and nervous (t...)
2 very beautiful; wonderful (s...)
3 strange and unusual (b...)
4 people who reach the last stage of a competition (f...)
5 not very happy (l... t... d...)
6 criticize strongly (c...)
7 short holiday by a couple immediately after their marriage (h...)
8 continue to exist (l...)

Improve your grammar

Sequence of adjectives

a General qualities come before particular ones
Example
creamy white silk dress

b Personal opinions go before more objective words
Example
stunning black car

c We usually use a maximum of three adjectives before a noun.

d Look at these examples.

opinion	size/ age/ shape	colour	origin	material	noun
stunning	full - length	ivory		silk	dress
	new	black	American		car

too and enough

e *too* goes before adjectives and adverbs and conveys the idea of 'more than is necessary'.
Example
This is too much.

f *enough* goes after adjectives and adverbs and conveys the idea of 'as much as is necessary'.
Example
We have enough problems.

Practice

4 Decide on the correct adjective order.

1 French/expensive/menu
2 silk/white/beautiful/wedding dress
3 gold/wedding rings/matching/two
4 attractive/name cards/pink
5 red/cushions/large
6 flat/new/beautiful
7 modern/wedding/British

5 Insert either *too* or *enough*:

1 It looked ____ beautiful to be real
2 I wasn't walking quickly ____ to catch up with them.
3 She was walking ____ quickly for me.
4 She is old ____ to marry.
5 They do not have ____ time.

6 Rewrite these sentences using *too* or *enough* so that they keep the same meaning.

1 She isn't old enough to get married.
   She's too _____.
2 I didn't have enough money for it all.
   I had too _____.
3 She wasn't tall enough to reach the cake.
   She was too _____.
4 I arrived too late to see the wedding.
   I didn't _____.

Talking point

7 Discuss what you need to make a marriage work? How important is love?

8 Look at these comments about the wedding you have just read about. Which do you agree with most? Why?

'Although they haven't met before, a lot of thought has been put into choosing the right people. You can't guarantee any marriage will be a happy one and this marriage has as much chance as any other.'

'It will never work.'

'I believe this competition is immoral, the media should not be offering prizes for getting married. Marriage is a serious commitment.'

'All the money and gifts in the world can't make two people fall in love.'

Listening

Modern weddings

9 Decide if these statements about marriage in Britain are true or false. Now listen and check your answers.

1 Marriage is not as popular as it was in the past.
2 Most people get married in a religious place.
3 Most brides wear white.
4 The bride's father normally pays for the wedding.
5 There are no arranged marriages in the UK.

Girls in school

Reading

1 Do you think girls learn better in single sex schools? Read the texts below and see if they support your ideas.

A

A recent survey of attitudes of teachers and students in mixed-sex classrooms revealed that over half of the boys believed that teachers favoured the girls. Interestingly, the girls were equally convinced that the teachers didn't favour them. In fact, many of the girls thought that the boys got more attention from the teachers because they were noisier. One of the girls said 'It may look like the girls get more attention because teachers enjoy talking to students who work hard and behave well, which is mainly the girls.' Interestingly, the survey also found high levels of confidence among the girls. Many of them admitted that they believed they were a lot more intelligent than the boys. More surprisingly, many of the boys agreed with them!

B

Boys don't benefit from single sex schools. The more boys there are the more unruly and violent they are. The pass rate of girls in single sex schools is higher than girls in mixed schools. However, the current trend for mixed schools suggests that mixed schools are thought of as 'better'. It seems that keeping boys happy is far more important than encouraging girls to do well in education. Unfortunately, the way that a lot of boys keep themselves happy is by turning sexual attention on the girls. 'Walk past a gang of boys in the corridors or outside and you can hear them making loud comments about you,'one girl said.

Inside the classrooms, researchers found that in general, boys ask more questions, misbehave more, and get more attention from the teachers. If there isn't enough apparatus in the science lesson, the boys grab it all. In English discussions, boys dominate the chat, even when there are fewer of them in the group. Despite this, girls do slightly better in all exam subjects.

2 Look back at the text and answer the questions.

1 According to the texts who benefits most from single sex schools?

2 The texts suggest a number of ways in which girls and boys are treated differently at school. Which ones do you agree with? Which would you reject? Why?

Vocabulary

3 What is the meaning of the expressions in **bold**? Give reasons for your answers.

1 **the pass rate**
   i the number of people who take an exam
   ii the number of people who succeed in an exam

2 The more **unruly** and violent
   i difficult to control
   ii angry

3 **the current trend**
   i general tendency or fashion
   ii movement downwards

4 **misbehave more**
   i are more unhappy
   ii are more frequently naughty

5 **enough apparatus**
   i equipment used in scientific experiments
   ii textbooks

Talking point

4 Discuss these questions using your own experience of school as evidence.

1 Are girls often upset by the behaviour and comments of boys, both in and out of class?
2 In your experience, do girls take considerably less part in lessons than boys?
3 Are certain subjects seen as girls' subjects?
4 Do you think the presence of the opposite sex contributes to poorer academic performance?

Improve your grammar

Modifying comparatives

a Words like *very*, *too* and *quite* can modify adjectives but not comparatives.
Example
He's very old. (**Not** *He's very older.*)

b To modify comparisons we can put a word or phrase (e.g. *slightly, a lot*) before a comparative to say how much quieter/better/more complicated/etc. something is.
Example
Are girls slightly better at exams than boys?
Girls are a lot quieter than boys.

The expressions we can use before a comparative include:
much, considerably, a lot, lots, far (= a large amount)
marginally, a little, slightly, a bit (= a small amount)
hardly any (= very, very little)

than me and *than I am*

After *than* or *as*, a personal pronoun on its own has the object form (e.g. *me*).
Example
You're older than me.
He isn't as clever as her.

But if the pronoun has a verb after it, then we use the subject form (e.g. *I*).
Example
You're older than I am.
He isn't as clever as she is.

6 Use the table to make ten true sentences. Include some comparatives and subjects of your own.

		slightly	shorter	
I	am	marginally	more intelligent	
My best friend	is	considerably	taller	
The boys in class	are	hardly any	better behaved	than
The girls in class	was	much	quieter	
The team	were	a little	better looking	
		a bit	better	

Practice

5 Complete the sentences with the correct form of the adjectives in brackets

1 Boys are so unsophisticated! All the girls I know are _____ than boys. (sophisticated)
2 He is a bit _____ than the other students. (bad)
3 She is considerably _____ than her sister. (young)
4 Her new school is a bit _____ than the old one so they will be able to save some money. (expensive)
5 He is so stupid! He is much _____ than his brother. (clever)
6 My sister is always studying. She is much _____ than I am. (hard-working)

Getting Streetwise! 📼

Moans and groans

7 Is there anything that you really hate? Listen to what some *New Streetwise* readers had to say and tick the expressions you hear

I can't stand ...
The thing that makes me cringe ...
What gets to me ...
My pet hate ...
I can't bear ...
I really loathe ...
I really hate ...
What I hate is ...
What really annoys me ...

8 Listen again. What do they hate?

9 Use the expressions you have just learnt to take part in a class survey of your pet hates.

The way we are

Warm-up

1 Do you feel you are a different person in different situations? Do you:

* speak differently when you are with different people? Who? When?
* argue with some people but not others? Who do you argue with? When?
* feel that you are more talkative with people your own age than with adults? Why?

Reading

2 Read these descriptions of Sue and try and match the descriptions to the writers.

Sue's younger brother
Sue's mother
Sue's father
Sue's best friend
Sue's boyfriend

Vocabulary

3 These adjectives can all be used to describe someone's personality.

shy	tense	polite
assertive	nervous	mean
aggressive	rude	selfish
frank	sensible	reliable
generous	sensitive	patient
easy-going	stubborn	ambitious

Which of these adjectives matches these definitions? If necessary, use a dictionary to help you.

1 understanding and aware of emotions
2 unwilling to spend money
3 speaking honestly and showing feelings openly
4 caring only about yourself
5 determined and unwilling to change your mind
6 not easily worried or upset by problems or other people's actions
7 able to make good decisions based on reason and not emotion
8 not polite
9 doesn't like talking to strangers or large groups of people

①

Sue has different ways of talking in different situations. Sometimes she will shout and scream at me and then the phone will ring and she answers it in this soft gentle voice.

②

I think girls should dress well but Sue isn't interested in fashion. She usually wears old jeans and a sweater. This makes her look really scruffy which is a shame because she's a pretty girl. I don't know when she'll start taking a pride in her appearance and start looking smart.

③

Sue's normally quite easy-going except when she screams at her brother and argues with her mum about the way she dresses. I just wish that she would talk to us and tell us more about her friends and what she does at school.

④

I met Sue about six months ago. She's great. She's gentle and has a good sense of humour. She's quite secretive, though, and rarely talks about her family.

⑤

Sue and I have been friends since we met in primary school. She always smiles and looks friendly. She's very easy-going and doesn't worry about life or the way she looks. I think that's why we get on.

Glossary

scruffy: *untidy*

smart: *well dressed, neat*

4 Divide the list of adjectives into those which are used to show approval and those which are used to show disapproval.

5 Look through the list and decide which ones describe you. Would your friends and family choose the same adjectives or different ones to describe you?

Improve your writing

Describing a person and their character

In order to provide an interesting description of a person, it is important to focus on their personality as well as their physical appearance.

a Use adjectives to describe their personality but provide examples that support your statements.

Examples

When we are with our parents he is shy and doesn't like talking about girls. When dad teases him his ears and cheeks turn bright red. At home Alan is quiet, but as soon as he meets up with friends he becomes so talkative that his friends often tell him to shut up.

She has a kind, smiley face and is always friendly and pleased to see you.

b We can link personality to physical appearance.

Examples

Alan is strong and well-built which makes him look quite tough, but in fact he is a quiet, sensitive person.

He is easy-going about lots of things, but he does worry about his appearance and his hair! He spends a lot of time in the bathroom trying to flatten his hair with water.

c We can also link personality to dress sense.

Example

Alan usually wears expensive sunglasses. He likes to look fashionable and cool.

Practice

6 Put the words into the correct order.

1 My uncle has short/hair/blond.
2 Alan has large/eyes/brown.
3 Karen has dark/long/eyelashes.
4 Peter has a scruffy/leather/jacket/brown.
5 He has a accent/Irish/lovely/soft.
6 Helen wore a stunning/dress/red/silk.

7 Complete the sentences about your own behaviour and mannerisms.

1 When I feel shy I _____.
2 When I am impatient I often _____.
3 When I am nervous I usually _____.
4 When my parents ask me what I have been doing I usually _____.
5 When I am out with my friends, I feel _____.

Writing

8 Follow the *Improve your writing* guidelines and write a description of yourself. Write it from the point of view of someone who knows you well, like a close friend or a member of your family. Do not use the first person (I) in your piece of writing. The description should show the different sides you present to the world, e.g. the way you speak to different people, the way you dress in different situations, etc.

Self check

9 Put the descriptions up on the classroom wall. Can you guess who the people are? Are there any ways you can improve the descriptions?

New Streetwise songbook

What can I do? 📼

I (1) _____ (not sleep) at all for days,
It (2) _____ (be) so long since we (3) _____
   (talk).
I (4) _____ (be) here many times,
I just (5) _____ (not know) what I (6) _____
   (do) wrong.

What can I do to make you love me?
What can I do to make you care?
What can I say to make you feel this?
What can I do to get you there?

There (7) _____ (be) only so much I can take,
And I've just got to let it go,
And who (8) _____ (know) I might feel better,
If I (9) _____ (not try) and I don't hope.

What can I do to make you love me?
What can I do to make you care?
What can I say to make you feel this?
What can I do to get you there?

No more waiting, no more aching,
No more fighting, no more trying.

Maybe there (10) _____ (be) nothing more
   to say,
And in a funny way I (11) _____ (be) calm,
Because the power (12) _____ (be) not mine,
I'm just going to let it fly.

What can I do to make you love me?
What can I do to make you care?
What can I say to make you feel this?
What can I do to get you there?

And love me?

1 Look at the song and put the verbs in brackets in the correct form.

2 Listen and check your answers.

3 Do you believe in love at first sight? Or that two people can learn to love each other? Why/Why not?

4 Discuss these questions in small groups and then share them with the class. Were your answers the same?
• What qualities might make you fall in love with someone?
• List five things a person could do to make a person fall in love with them.
• Can you think of things a person shouldn't do if they want someone to fall in love with them?

Friends

Is there anything you wouldn't do to help a friend?

Music power

Where and when do you listen to music?

It's only a game

What are these young people doing? Have you ever done anything similar? Where? When?

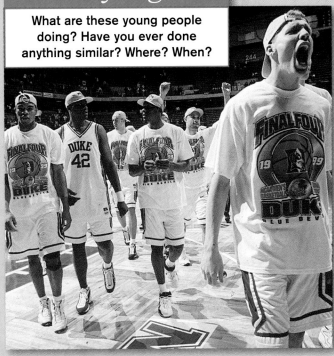

Friends

Reading 📼

1 Read the text and answer the questions.

1 What is the dilemma for the reader?
2 What would you do in this situation?

Graffiti has suddenly appeared on your university buildings. It seems to be the work of one graffiti artist but nobody has owned up and admitted responsibility. The university is famous for its old and beautiful buildings and the graffiti is very unattractive.

One day you call in on your friend to borrow a book. He is out, and his mother asks you to wait in his room. While you wait for him to turn up you start looking at his books. You come across a box on his book shelf which is full of aerosol paints and graffiti designs. You knew your friend liked art but you didn't imagine he could be the graffiti artist.

If you turn him in, you will lose a friend and cause trouble for his family – he already has enough trouble with his dad. On the other hand, if you turn a blind eye, you'll be letting your university down and the buildings will continue to be damaged. If you tell someone you think you know who the mystery graffiti artist is you'll be drawn in and you don't really want to get involved.

What would you do?

Glossary

to turn a blind eye: *to purposefully ignore something that you know is wrong*

Vocabulary

2 Match the verbs you have found in the text with these definitions.

1 to visit (on the way to somewhere else)
2 to find something or someone by chance
3 to become involved (in something)
4 to take someone to the police
5 to admit to a crime
6 to arrive (often unexpectedly)

3 Match these phrasal verbs with their definitions.

put up with
stick up for
split up
look up to
get on (with)

1 support or defend someone, oneself, etc.
2 end a relationship (with someone)
3 respect and admire someone
4 tolerate or accept a situation that is unsatisfactory
5 to have a friendly relationship with someone

Improve your grammar

Phrasal verbs

A phrasal verb is a verb + preposition/adverb particle combination. The combination usually has a different meaning from the words used separately.

a Which of these examples is a phrasal verb?
  1 When he looked into the room he saw nobody.
  2 The police looked into the mystery of the missing diamonds.

b Read the text and find all the phrasal verbs. Write them down in the infinitive form.
  Example
  to call someone in

Practice

4 Complete these sentences with a phrasal verb from the vocabulary exercises.

1 He was late. He didn't _____ until ten o'clock'.
2 'Have you found the letter?' 'Yes, I was lucky. I _____ it yesterday.'
3 I _____ with James really well. He's my best friend.
4 I _____ to see my granddad on my way home from school.
5 I always _____ my friends, even if I sometimes disagree with them.

5 Substitute the verbs in **bold** with a suitable phrasal verb.

1 She really **respects** and **admires** her best friend.
2 They have decided to **investigate** the problem.
3 They **ended** their relationship when they went to different universities.
4 Splitting up with Sam was really difficult but I have **recovered** now.
5 I **tolerated** her bad manners because I loved her.

Pronunciation 🔊

Sentence stress

6 The verb and the preposition/particle in phrasal verbs are usually stressed. Pronouns between the verb and the preposition/particle are not stressed.
Decide how you would read these pairs of sentences.

1 He turned in his friend.
  He turned him in.
2 It'll draw you in.
  You'll be drawn in.

7 Listen and repeat.

Talking point

8 Look at the recipe for a happy friendship and discuss these questions in small groups.

1 Which do you think are the most important ingredients? Why? Agree on their order of importance starting with the most important.
2 What other ingredients for a happy friendship can you think of?

A recipe for a happy friendship

1 Make time to see your best friend. School work, boy/girl friends, and families can get in the way.

2 Listen to your friend's problems.

3 Don't leave your friend out of new friendships, hobbies, or interests.

4 Don't talk about your friend to other people. He/she will be very hurt when he/she finds out what you've been saying.

5 Learn to apologize. It is important to be able to admit that you are wrong.

6 Always give your friend time to be alone if she/he wants it.

Listening 🔊

9 Listen to Max, Hetty, John, and Sophie talking about problems with their friends. Which ingredient in the friendship recipe are they talking about?

1 Max

_____

2 Hetty

_____

3 John

_____

4 Sophie

_____

Music power

Warm-up 📼

1 Listen to the tape. Follow the instructions and answer the questions.

1 What effect did the music on tape have on you?
2 What kind of music did you hear in the warm-up exercise? Is it the type of music you usually listen to or not?

Reading 📼

2 Read the text and put in these paragraph headings.

Music and plants
Music for healing
The effect of music
Music all around us

The power of music

1 _____
Nowadays it's almost impossible to escape from music, even if we want to. It thunders out of every high-street shop, hisses horribly from other people's stereos on public transport, and blasts out of open car windows.

2 _____
Although many of us enjoy music, very few of us have any real idea of the effect music has on us. Most people assume that musical tastes are subjective – that one person will like jazz while another prefers classical. In fact, recent research in America and Australia has shown that appreciation of music is not a matter of individual taste. Certain types of music will have a particular effect on our minds and bodies, whether we like them or not. For instance, early classical music will help us feel relaxed and peaceful. Other types of classical music, such as the music of J.S. Bach and Mozart, are stimulating to the brain, encouraging curiosity and alertness. While classical music promotes loving feelings, hard rock music is a particularly good example of music that makes us feel hate, jealousy, and violence.

3 _____
As a result of this research, music is being used in hospitals, and doctors have found that 20 minutes of soothing music is often far more effective than tranquillizers. For example, after a recent operation, Fiona Richmond was not allowed to listen to her favourite heavy metal group. Instead, she was made to listen to gentle classical music because it was good for her.

4 _____
Scientific work on the healing power of music started with plant research in the 1970s. Interestingly, many types of classical music speeded plant growth, whereas heavy metal caused plants to draw away from the speakers and die.

3 Read the text again. Are these statements true or false?

1 Our taste in music is personal.
2 Music can affect us physically.
3 The only music which affects us positively is music that we like.
4 Music can be used to cure people in hospitals.
5 Certain types of music can be harmful.

Vocabulary 🔲

4 The following adjectives are often used to describe music. Match them with their opposites.

loud	discordant
joyful	modern
gentle	harsh
soothing	depressing
violent	exciting
happy	peaceful
traditional	sad
harmonious	quiet

5 Now listen to four pieces of music. Use the adjectives to describe them. Which ones did you like?

Talking point

6 Discuss these questions in a small group.

1 Do you believe rock music can be harmful? Why/Why not?
2 What music would you listen to in hospital after a serious operation? Why?

Improve your grammar
....

make, let, and allowed to

a If we make someone do something, we force them to do it. If we want to use *make* in the passive in this sense we must add *to*.
Example
Active He *made* her listen to Beethoven when she was younger.
Passive She was *made to* listen to Beethoven when she was younger.

b We cannot use *let* in the passive. Instead, we have to use *allowed to*.
Example
Active The doctors did not *let* her listen to loud music.
Passive She was not *allowed to* listen to loud music.
(Not ~~She wasn't let to listen ...~~)

Practice

7 Complete these sentences with an appropriate form of *make, let, or allow*.

1 When I was a boy my father ____ me listen to classical music. I hated it.
2 ____ you ____ to go out alone at night when you were younger?
3 His father usually ____ him listen to pop music while he does his homework. My father doesn't ____ me.
4 My mother used to ____ me go to bed at nine.
5 He wants to go. Why don't you ____ him?
6 I was ____ to eat carrots. I still dislike them.

8 Make as many sentences as you can about these situations using *make, let*, and *allow*.

1 Fiona did not want to listen to classical music but the doctors insisted.
2 Alan wanted to play in a rock band but his father told him he couldn't.
3 Alice wanted to go to the disco but her mother told her she had to finish her homework first.
4 Chris did not like piano lessons but his parents told him to go.
5 His teachers gave him permission to play the electric guitar in music lessons.
6 Sandra has to wear headphones to listen to heavy metal.

Getting Streetwise! 🔲
Permission

9 When we need to ask permission, the words we choose will depend on who we are speaking to, the amount of resistance we expect, etc.
Look at each of these situations. How polite would you have to be? What would you say?

1 You are visiting friends with your parents. An important basketball match is on television. You want to watch it.
2 You are staying with friends. You want to phone your parents who are in New York.
3 You are by the pool with a friend. You want to use their sun cream.

Now listen to the extracts and answer the questions.

1 What expressions were used to ask permission? Which of these was the most formal? Which was the most informal?
2 What expressions did the speakers use to give permission?
3 What was used to refuse permission?

It's only a game

Warm-up

1 Have you got a favourite basketball or football team? Do you ever go to live basketball or football matches? Why/Why not?

Reading

2 Read this article about the fans of an American College basketball team and put in the missing expressions.

When the game starts at one
For example, last month
Whenever the team song is played
Whenever the other team
At eleven the doors open
By seven o'clock
While they wait

The craziest basketball fans in the world?

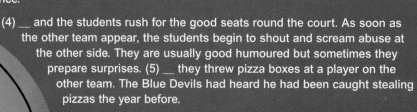

The Duke University home game last Saturday was as crazy and colourful as ever. Basketball is a passion for the students at Duke University in the USA. The Duke basketball team and its fans are called the Blue Devils and when they play at home the day starts early. (1) __ there is a long line of students waiting to get into the College stadium. (2) __ , they paint slogans onto posters and bed sheets. Some students put on blue wigs. Others put blue paint on their faces and bodies and some stand there sleepily and eat breakfast. (3) __ on one of the portable CD players, the queue begins to dance.

(4) __ and the students rush for the good seats round the court. As soon as the other team appear, the students begin to shout and scream abuse at the other side. They are usually good humoured but sometimes they prepare surprises. (5) __ they threw pizza boxes at a player on the other team. The Blue Devils had heard he had been caught stealing pizzas the year before.

(6) __ the Blue Devils roar encouragement to their team. (7) __ have a foul, they do what they can to put their opponents off. They wave their arms in the air or move from left to right behind the basket. They shout as the ball is about to be released or most, effectively, they sit in silence. Once they turned their backs and sang 'It just doesn't matter'. Their opponent missed.

When The Blue Devils win, their opponents leave quickly. But the Duke fans stay and celebrate on the court. They hug each other and they finally stop screaming.

Practice

3 Complete this text with appropriate expressions from the list below. Note that there are more expressions than you need.

the night before   a few hours before
a few minutes before   after   the start of
before   at the end of   until
a few minutes after

The FA (Football Association) Cup Final

The English FA Cup final is played in Wembley stadium in North London. Most teams spend (1) _____ the game in hotels near the ground. (2) _____ kick-off, they take the short bus journey to the stadium. The players like to walk on the pitch and sample the atmosphere (3) _____ they change into their football kit. As (4) _____ the game approaches the crowd gets noisier and noisier. The crowd usually does a lot of singing. Members of the royal family usually attend and (5) _____ the game starts, they are introduced to both teams. The teams then get a chance for a little practice (6) _____ it is time for the referee to start the game.

Vocabulary

4 Match the words from the texts with the definitions.

foul   the other side   a passion   effectively
portable   kick off

1 the opposite team
2 succesfully
3 start of the game
4 strong feelings
5 easily moveable
6 against the rules of a sport

Improve your writing

Writing an article about an event

a Try to think of a catchy title that will interest the reader. Your opening sentence should follow on from the title and make the reader want to read on.

b Organize your work into paragraphs. Put related points together and each new point into a new paragraph. When describing an event, you may wish to have paragraphs for what happens before, during, and after the event.

c It is important to describe what happens in sequence. These expressions can help:
*at/by seven o'clock   the day before/after
in the morning/afternoon/evening
at the start/end of the day
as soon as/when/after/before*

d Decide on your style before you begin. This depends on the subject you are writing about and who will be reading it. An article can be light-hearted and entertaining or serious.

e Include details about the atmosphere of the event, the mood of the participants (what do they wear/do/etc?) that will keep the reader interested.

f Think about what your reader knows. For example, will you need to explain any technical terms or non-English words?

g Check your tenses. If you are writing about a specific happening that you attended, then use past tenses. If you are writing about something more general or something that usually happens use present tenses.

Writing

5 Follow the *Improve your writing* guidelines to write an article about an important national occasion – for example a cup final, a festival, or another event. You should assume you are writing for someone from another culture. Try to be informative and entertaining.

Self check

6 Work in a small group and look through the articles you have written. Give a mark from 1–5 for each of these areas.
• Did the articles use appropriate paragraphing?
• Did they make the sequence of events clear?
• Did they have a range of structures and vocabulary?

Grammar review

Issues 7 and 8

Sequence of adjectives

When we use more than one adjective with a noun we have to take care with the word order. There are no absolute rules, since a lot depends on the emphasis a speaker wishes to make. Here is a general guide:

opinion	size/age/shape	colour	origin	material	noun
beautiful	large	red	Japanese	velvet	dress
stunning	new	gold			chairs
	square				table

1 General qualities come before particular ones.
   Example
   creamy white sponge cake

2 Personal opinions go before more objective words.
   Example
   beautiful tall building

3 Size generally precedes age and shape, etc.
   Examples
   a big old house
   a small round table

Notes
Adjectival past participles are usually closest to the noun.
a handmade sweater
an outdated telephone book
an elevated railway

We usually use a maximum of two or three adjectives before the noun, adding extra details afterwards.
gold-plated telephone cards, personalized with the guest's name

Too and enough

1 *too* goes before adjectives and adverbs, and conveys the idea of 'more than is necessary' or 'excess'. Do not confuse this with the intensifier *very* which does not have the idea of 'excess'.
   Examples
   It looked too beautiful to be real.
   My father works too hard.
   The bride was very beautiful. (**Not** ... ~~too beautiful~~)

2 *enough* can come after adjectives and adverbs. It means that the person can or can't do the thing that is mentioned because of their age, speed, etc.

Examples
She is old enough to marry.
I wasn't fast enough to catch up with them.

It can also come before nouns to express the idea of 'as much as you need'.
Examples
They do not have enough time to do the exercise.
I've had enough cake, thank you.

Comparatives and modifiers

Words like *very, too* and *quite* can modify adjectives, e.g. *very tall, too young, quite old,* but not comparatives.
He's very old. (**Not** ~~He's very older.~~)
To modify comparisons we use expressions like *much, far, a lot, lots, rather, hardly any, a little, a bit,* etc.
Examples
It's much/a little/a bit colder than yesterday.
Prices are much/a little higher in New York.
He is hardly any/a little bit taller than his brother.

Expressions like *considerably, marginally, slightly* provide for degrees of comparison.
The pass rate in mixed schools is considerably lower.

We can also use *no* + comparative to emphasize similarity or to show there has been no change.
Examples
Peter is a terrible tennis player, and his brother is no better.
'Is your uncle still in hospital?' 'Yes, I'm afraid he's no better.'

Phrasal verbs

Form
verb + preposition/adverb particle (e.g. *down, up, out, after,* etc.)
Some phrasal verbs require an object (i.e. are 'transitive').

	verb	object	preposition/adverb particle
I	*picked*	*the letter*	*up.*
He	*let*	*his brother*	*down.*

Others cannot take an object (i.e. are 'intransitive').

	verb	preposition/adverb particle
Their marriage	*broke*	*down.*
The plane	*took*	*off.*

Meaning

1 In some cases the meaning of the phrasal verb is clear from the verb + preposition/adverb particle combination.
Example
He put the picture up on the outside wall.

2 Sometimes the combination has a special meaning.
Example
He puts up with a lot. (= tolerates or accepts an unpleasant situation)

Word order

1 When the verb takes an object, the preposition/adverb particle can come:
1 before the object, e.g. *He picked up the letter.*
2 after the object, e.g. *He picked the letter up.*

2 If the object is very long, it comes after the particle.
Example
He picked up the letter and the envelopes that were with it.

3 If the object is a pronoun (e.g. *them*, *it*, etc.) it usually comes before the particle.
Example
He picked them up. (**Not** *He picked up them.*)

However, some phrasal verbs take an object but we do not separate them from the particle.
Example
My uncle looked after me as a child. (**Not** ... *looked me after* ...)

Make, let, allow

Make

1 If we make someone or something do something, we force them to do it. We need an object.

2 *make* in the active is followed by infinitive without *to*.

Examples
He made her listen to Beethoven when she was younger.
He made me move my car.

3 *make* in the passive is followed by infinitive with *to*.

Examples
She was made to listen to Beethoven when she was younger.
I was made to move my car.

Let and *allow*

1 If you let or allow someone to do something, especially someone you have authority over, you give them permission or do not try to stop them.

Examples
After thinking about it, my father let me take driving lessons.
I was allowed to go provided I was home by 11.

2 *Let* is followed by infinitive without *to* in the active. *Let* does not have a passive form and is replaced by *allowed to*.

Examples
Active: *My parents let me go to the disco.*
Passive: *I was allowed to go to the disco.*
(**Not** ~~I was let go to the disco.~~)

Grammar practice

A ....

1 Complete the sentences with an appropriate comparative or superlative form of the adjectives in brackets. Make any additions you need.

Examples
I am *younger than* my sister. (young)
He isn't as *old as* he looks. (old)
They are the *best* in the class. (good)

1 Which is the _____ city in your country? (large)
2 His writing is as _____ mine. (bad)
3 Who is the _____ student in class? (serious)
4 The bride was as _____ he was. (tall)
5 She is one of the _____ people I know. (attractive)
6 The cakes were as _____ the sandwiches. (good)
7 He was _____ his brother. (short)
8 He has the _____ house from the school. (far)

2 Complete the sentences with *too* or *enough* and an adjective from the box.

hot sweet old fast late loud expensive

1 I can't drink this! It's _____ .
2 He's only fifteen. He isn't _____ to drive.
3 He hasn't won any races this year. His car isn't _____ .
4 I didn't have enough money to buy it. It was _____ .
5 'We can't hear the TV.' 'Sorry, isn't it _____ ?'
6 I'm afraid we were _____ to catch the plane.
7 Could I have some more sugar please? It's not _____ .

3 Put *to* into the blanks only if it's necessary.

1 I allowed him ____ go.
2 She let her daughter ____ stay out till midnight.
3 He made him ____ stand outside for the whole lesson.
4 I wasn't allowed ____ watch the programme on TV.
5 Did she let you ____ borrow her cassettes?
6 He always makes me ____ wait for him.
7 She was made ____ wear those shoes.
8 My mum never lets me ____ go to films alone.
9 The film was very funny. It made me ____ laugh.
10 My older brother used to make me ____ cry.

B ···

1 Rewrite these sentences so that they keep the same meaning

1 She isn't old enough to vote.
  She is too _____ .
2 I didn't have enough time to finish.
  I had too _____ .
3 She was too young to go in.
  She wasn't _____ .
4 He's rich enough to own a plane.
  He's not too _____ .
5 The weather was too cold to swim.
  The weather wasn't _____ .

2 Decide on the best word-order.

Example
tiny Japanese computer new a
a tiny new Japanese computer

1 short hair brown horrible
2 plastic shoes cheap
3 middle-aged a man handsome
4 cakes small round three
5 beautiful dress blue a
6 plate attractive an old handpainted
7 young an woman Irish intelligent

3 Complete the following sentences with one word.

Example
Look! There's something on the floor. Pick it *up*!

1 The music is too soft. Turn it ____ .
2 Why don't you give ____ smoking? It's bad for you.
3 He was walking in the street when he came ____ ten dollars.
4 The police said they would look ____ the thefts.
5 I'm looking ____ my lost keys.
6 Who looked ____ you as a child?
7 My sister doesn't see him any more. They broke ____ two weeks ago.

4 Replace the words in italics with a pronoun.

Example
Do you get on with *the Smiths*?
Do you get on with them?

1 He let *his friends* down.
2 I called in on *my aunt* on the way home.
3 I don't want to put up with *Sally's* rudeness any more.
4 They put *the building* up in less than a week.
5 He hasn't got over *the match* yet.

5 Use *make*, *let*, and *allow* to write a sentence for each of these situations.

Example
Sara wanted to go to a pop concert. Her father said she couldn't go because she hadn't finished her homework.
He made her stay at home.
He didn't let her go to the concert.
She wasn't allowed to go.

1 The teacher told the class that they had to stay behind until they had all finished the exercise.
2 Alice wanted to go to the cinema but her mother told her to stay at home and help her with the housework.
3 Alice's brother is doing military service. He had long hair before, but it is now very short.
4 Tom was very tired after doing thirty lengths of the swimming pool, but his coach told him to do ten more.

C ···

1 A pen friend is thinking of buying her brother either a dog or a cat as a pet. She has asked your opinion on which is better. Use the words below as part of your answer.

intelligent   well-behaved   gentle   obedient   a lot
independent   clean   aggressive   a little   much

2 Use all the words below to describe the furniture in the pictures.

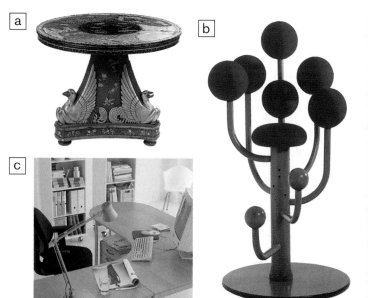

modern   old   Chinese   table   uncomfortable
office   chair   desk   wooden   valuable   attractive

3 You are writing to a pen friend. Use *make*, *let*, and *allow* to write a short paragraph describing how the adults in your house treat you.

New Streetwise

Explorers

What do you think this man is doing?

If only...

Do you always use the proper safety equipment? Why/Why not?

Teenage sports stars

Are sports stars getting younger? Give reasons for your answers.

Explorers

Warm-up

1 Look at the pictures. Which is the greatest achievement? Why?

Reading 📼

2 Read the text quickly and answer these questions.

1 Why is Peter Simmons a good explorer?
2 Why do you make slow progress when you walk to the North Pole?
3 What is an unsupported walk?
4 How did Tom Reeves find Peter?
5 Why wouldn't Peter's trip have counted?
6 Why did Peter give up after he had helped Tom?

Going around the world in a balloon

Walking to the Pole

Walking to the Pole

Peter Simmons is one of the world's most accomplished explorers. Peter has climbed the highest mountains in six of the seven continents and walked to both the South and North Poles.

Peter feels his greatest achievement was the unsupported walk he did to the North Pole. Walking to the North Pole is full of dangers. The moving ice cap moves backwards almost as fast as than you can walk forwards so when you rest, you drift backwards. Much of the time is spent walking over the frozen sea. Thin ice and polar bears can be a problem. On an unsupported walk you have to take your own supplies and you cannot get help from anyone.

The first time Peter tried to walk to the North Pole there was an incident in which another British Explorer, Tom Reeves, would have died if he hadn't come across Peter's camp. Reeves was lost on a separate expedition but luckily he saw Peter's tracks in the snow. He only had hours to live and Peter is sure that Reeves would have died if he hadn't helped him. Peter fed Reeves, warmed him up, and radioed for a plane to come to his rescue. Peter knew that helping Reeves put his own trip in danger. The weather was getting warmer and every minute he spent waiting for the plane put him in danger from melting ice. He also knew that there was a possibility that his trip wouldn't count because he had been in contact with the outside world. Only a few hours later, Peter dropped through the ice into the Arctic Ocean. He was rescued but did not reach the North Pole until a year later on another expedition.

Climbing Everest

Vocabulary

3 Find words in the text that mean:

1 skilled, good at something (a...)
2 the seven large land masses in the world (c...)
3 something you have succeeded in (a...)
4 without help (u...)
5 move slowly, without effort (d...)
6 essential food and equipment (s...)
7 unusual event (i...)
8 turning to liquid (m...)

Improve your grammar

Third conditional

The form of third conditional is
If + past perfect + *would have* + past participle
Example
If Reeves hadn't come across Peter's camp, he would have died.
We use this structure to talk about an event that did not happen because of an event in the *if* clause. Can we tell from this sentence whether Reeves died or not?

Practice

4 Complete the sentences with the past perfect of the words in brackets, or with *would/wouldn't have* + past participle.

1 If he hadn't fallen into the sea, Peter __ (got) to the North Pole.
2 Reeves would have died if Peter __ (not help) him.
3 Peter __ (felt) very guilty if he had let the Reeves die.
4 Reeves __ (get) home if he hadn't been rescued by plane.
5 I would have helped Reeves if I __ (be) there.
6 Peter __ (accept) help, if they had offered him some.
7 They __ (climb) to the top of Everest if the weather hadn't changed.
8 I would have screamed if I __ (see) a polar bear.

5 Write a sentence in the third conditional for each of these situations.

Example
Reeves was rescued because he found Peter's camp.
If he hadn't found Peter's camp, he wouldn't have been rescued.

1 Peter did not die because he had warm clothing.
If he hadn't _____ .
2 Peter was able to explore the North Pole because he had a lot of money.
If Peter hadn't had _____ .
3 He fell into the sea because the ice was thin.
If the ice _____ .
4 They made slow progress because the ice moved backwards.
If the ice _____ .
5 Peter was rescued because he had a satellite phone.
If he hadn't _____ .
6 He called for help because he had no supplies.
If he _____ .

Listening

6 Can you name any famous women explorers? Why do you think there are so few?
Listen to a *New Streetwise* report on women explorers and answer these questions.

1 How does the report explain why there haven't been many women explorers in the past?
2 Match these women explorers to their achievements.

Eileen Collins	The first woman to climb Mount Everest
Freya Stark	The first woman in space
Valentina Tereshkova	Travelled in the Mountains of Iran
Junko Tabei	The first woman commander of a space shuttle
Ann Bancroft	The first woman to travel across ice to the North Pole

7 Listen again and decide which of these women:

• was buried by an avalanche
• was sent in the wrong direction
• would have crossed a continent
• was in the American air force
• was a teacher

Pronunciation

Word stress

8 Listen to the way these words are pronounced and mark the stress. Identify the weak form /ə/ where it occurs.

explorer   generation
exploration   competitor
expedition   competition

Listen and repeat.

Talking point

9 Which of these views do you agree with most? Why? Share your answers with the class.

1 The golden age of exploration is over. There are no more great adventures left on our planet.
2 The golden age of exploration is here. We are beginning to find out more about the world and its mysteries.
3 The golden age of exploration hasn't happened yet. We know nothing about the secrets of the universe.

If only ...

Warm-up

1 What is the law on car seat belts and motorcycle helmets in your country? Carry out a class survey and find out how many students wouldn't:
- use a seat-belt in the front of a car.
- use a seat-belt in the back of a car.
- wear a helmet on a motorcycle.
- wear a helmet while riding a bicycle.

Reading

2 Work in pairs. Before you read the text decide if these statements are true or false.

1 Most people killed in cycling accidents were not wearing a helmet.
2 Bicycle helmets cut down on the risk of head injury.
3 In the UK most cyclists wear helmets.
4 Cyclists are less likely to suffer head injuries than motorcyclists.
5 A fall at low speeds can't kill.

3 Now check your answers by reading the text as quickly as possible.

What price a cycle helmet

On a rainy November morning two years ago, Shirley Huxham was free-wheeling gently downhill. As she waved to a friend, her bike skidded on the wet road, throwing her to the ground.

'I'd never even thought of buying a helmet,' she says. For months she was partly paralysed down her left side and still has health problems today.

Last year, 12-year-old James Dowson was riding his new mountain bike on a woodland track near his home. He hurtled down a steep slope and up the other side but lost control of his bike. James hit his head on a tree.

'My injuries started where my bike helmet stopped,' says James. His helmet had saved his life.

Some might think that James and Shirley were just unlucky. How dangerous can it be to fall from a bicycle?

Each year on Britain's roads more than 200 people are killed and at least 4,000 seriously injured on bicycles. But these numbers don't tell the whole story: the majority of the dead and injured were not wearing protective helmets.

A study of bicycle accidents in the US found that helmets reduced the risk of serious head injury by 85 per cent. Yet it is estimated that less than five per cent of British cyclists wear helmets. Why don't more cyclists wear them? There are a variety of reasons.

People think that helmets look foolish, that they're inconvenient, and that accidents only happen to other people.

One of the biggest misconceptions among bicycle riders is that lower speeds put cyclists at less risk than motorcyclists, who are legally obliged to wear helmets. In fact, according to a British report, a higher percentage of bicyclists than motorcyclists suffer head injuries. And their injuries can be just as severe.

Protective headgear, however, can make all the difference. James wasn't just lucky. If he hadn't worn a helmet, he would be dead, and if Shirley had, she wouldn't have spent months in hospital. Why take the risk?

Glossary

free-wheeling: *travelling on a bicycle without using the pedals*

woodland track: *rough pathway through woods*

Vocabulary

4 Find words in the text which mean:

1 slide (s...)
2 not able to move part of your body (p...)
3 damage to the body (i...)
4 travelled very fast (h...)
5 silly (f...)
6 a wrong idea about something (m...)
7 the possibility of danger or coming to harm (r...)
8 serious (s...)

Improve your grammar

Third conditional with a present outcome

a We can use this form to talk about the imagined present outcome or result of an imagined past action.

If clause	main clause
past perfect (imagined condition)	*would* + infinitive (present outcome)
If I had been careful,	*I wouldn't be in hospital now.*

Examples
If Shirley had worn a helmet two years ago, she wouldn't have health problems now. (But she didn't wear one, so she has problems.)
If I had had some sleep last night, I wouldn't be so tired today. (But I didn't, so I am tired.)

b We use *wish* or *if only* + past perfect to express regret for something that has or hasn't happened.
Examples
I wish I had learned to play the guitar.
If only I had worn my seat-belt.

Practice

5 Write a sentence for each situation using the third conditional with a present outcome.

Example
Simon was not wearing a helmet when he fell off his bike. He is in hospital.
If he had been wearing a helmet, he wouldn't be in hospital now.

1 James was wearing a helmet when he hit the tree. He is alive.
2 The government introduced a seat-belt law. My cousin now wears one.
3 I read an article about cycle safety. I now wear a cycle helmet.

4 The man who knocked a cyclist down is now in jail.
5 My uncle is now very rich. He started a factory which makes safety-helmets.
6 Fiona went skiing. She broke her leg and can't walk.

6 Complete these sentences with a present outcome.

1 If I hadn't started to learn English, _____ .
2 If I hadn't come to school today, _____ .
3 If we hadn't invented the motor car, _____ .
4 If we hadn't built all these tourist hotels, _____ .
5 If computers had been invented in the nineteenth century, _____ .

7 Complete these expressions of regret with an appropriate verb phrase using the present perfect.

Example
My team lost the championship in the last match.
If only they had won the last match they would have won the championship.

1 I failed my exam because I was late. I wish
_____ .
2 My friends won the lottery but I didn't join them. If only _____ .
3 My grandmother didn't know the table was valuable when she sold it. She wishes
_____ .
4 I didn't get the job because I couldn't speak English. If only _____ .

Getting Streetwise! 📼

Expressing regrets

8 Listen to extracts from four different interviews. In each case the interviewee is expressing regret about something that she or he did or didn't do.

1 What is each person expressing regret about?
2 What expressions did they use to express regret?

9 Work in pairs and write a dialogue in which you interview someone about their past regrets. Be ready to show your dialogue to the class.

Teenage sports stars

Reading

1 Read the texts and answer the questions. Which extract suggests that:
- training can harm young people?
- winning has become too important?
- training too hard can ruin a sporting career?

a

People used to argue that sports promoted discipline and a sense of fair play. Today, many people think that the emphasis on winning has become a problem. According to *Seventeen* magazine 'Winning becomes more important than honesty, schoolwork, health, happiness and most other important aspects of life.'

b

For many young people sport is no longer a game of basketball at lunchtime or a game of tennis at the weekend, but a serious and expensive business involving hours of daily training. For some, that training starts at a very early age, which is why more and more world champions are in their teens. However, recent studies suggest that overtraining can lead to stunted growth, injuries, and eating disorders in young people.

c

Marta Neil is only nineteen. If things had worked out as planned, Marta would be playing in this year's Wimbledon tennis championships. Instead, she'll be watching the championships on television. Marta had to give up a promising tennis career because of an injury which could have been prevented with proper rest between matches. Marta's story illustrates the competitiveness of modern sport and the damaging effect this can have on young people.

Glossary

stunted: *prevented from growing to full height*

eating disorders: *psychological illnesses which affect diet and weight*

fair play: *playing by the rules*

Improve your writing

Writing an opinion piece

a Start by listing ideas for and against your topic.

b It is important to have a strong introductory paragraph to start your opinion piece. You can start by presenting the opposite point of view to your own.
Examples
People used to think …
Some people argue …
According to …

Follow this with linking words such as *but, however,* or *on the other hand* to introduce your/the other side of the argument.

c Organize what you want to say into main topic areas and have a paragraph for each topic. Start each new paragraph with a sentence that introduces the main topic of the paragraph.
Examples
Another problem is that money has become too important …
A problem with sports today is that people are too competitive …

You can link additional ideas to the main topic by using expressions like *Furthermore,* and *In addition.*

d You can personalize the argument by using real life examples to support your argument.
Example
Karen Stevens is 17. If she had …

e Make sure you bring the argument to a conclusion and finish your opinion piece with a summary of your opinions.
Examples
In conclusion …
To sum up …

Practice

2 Use the word in brackets to write a sentence that introduces the main idea of each of these paragraphs.

1 (cheating) _____
Since the jobs of professionals depend on winning, they often do practically anything to win. An example of this ...

2 (spectators) _____
They are often obscene and violent, and fights are common at sporting events. Even at home ...

3 (injuries) _____
Sadly most of these involve children who are introduced early in life to highly competitive sport. Medical evidence suggests ...

3 Complete the sentences with one of these linking words.

Furthermore/In addition   However (x2)

1 Some people believe that footballers make too much money. _____ they have a short career and so don't earn this much money for very long.

2 Drugs in sport have always been a problem. _____ making sport less competitive will not stop drug taking because people always want to win.

3 Many people believe that success in sport is easy. _____ you have to work hard for it. _____ you sometimes pay a high price for success. Many sports men and women suffer from poor health when they get older.

Vocabulary

4 Match the names of these sports to the pictures.

volleyball   weight-lifting   fishing
table tennis   gymnastics   archery
badminton   riding

5 Which do you think is the odd one out? Why?

1 compete   train   race   play
2 wrestling   fencing   athletics   hunting
3 tired   depressed   stressed   injured

Talking point

6 Look at these opinions on sport today. Which ones do you agree with? Why/Why not?

- There's too much sport on television.
- Sportsmen and women make too much money.
- Winning has become too important. Look at the number of people who take drugs.
- Events like the Olympics are too expensive.
- Sport has become something for the rich.
- People take sport far too seriously. Just look at the behaviour of football fans.

Writing

7 Choose one of the opinions in *Talking point* and use it as the title of an opinion piece. Follow the *Improve your writing* guidelines to help you.

Self check

8 Read your partner's opinion piece. Give a mark each time they use linking words and a sentence that introduces the main topic of a new paragraph. Who had the most marks?

New Streetwise songbook

(Everything I do) I do it for you

Look into my eyes, you will see
(1) _____
Search your heart, search your soul
and when you find me there,
(2) _____
Don't tell me it's not worth trying for,
(3) _____
You know it's true, everything I do, I do it
  for you.
(4) _____
there's nothing there to hide.
Take me as I am, take my life.
I could give it all, I would sacrifice.
Don't tell me it's not worth fighting for.

I can't help it, there's nothing I want more.
(5) _____
There's no love like your love,
(6) _____
There's nowhere unless you're there,
all the time, all the way, yeah.
Oh you can't tell me it's not worth trying for.
I can't help it, there's nothing I'd want more.
Yeah, I would fight for you,
(7) _____
Walk the wire for you,
Yeah, I'd die for you.
You know it's true, everything I do, I do it
  for you.

1 Share what you know about Robin Hood. Do you have characters like him in your country?

2 Look at this song from a film about Robin Hood and replace the missing lines. Listen and check your answers.

  you'll search no more
  you can't tell me it's not worth dying for.
  what you mean to me
  Look into your heart, you will find,
  You know it's true, everything I do, I do it for you.
  and no other could give more love.
  I'd lie for you,

3 Do you think this is a good song for the film? Why/Why not?

4 This song became very popular with millions of people who
did not see the film? Do you like the song? Why?/Why not?

5 What other songs or music have become popular because of
a film?

ISSUE 10

NEW Streetwise

Astrology
Why do some people consult astrologers?

A gap year
What are these young people doing?

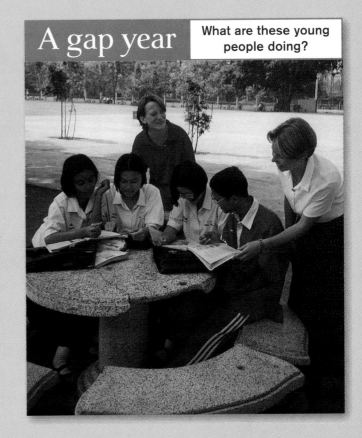

Pop music
How important is pop music in your life?

Astrology

1 Do you read the horoscopes in newspapers and magazines?

Hooked on horoscopes

Why do so many people believe in, and sometimes act on the predictions of astrologers? Astrology has no scientific evidence to support it yet people from all backgrounds consult their horoscopes every day.

Psychologists suggest that one answer may be the Barnum Effect. This is the term used to describe how people will believe feedback about their personality, when they think it's the result of a proper procedure.

The Barnum Effect works well when people receive feedback they believe is specific to them. For example, a French astrologer sent out detailed computer horoscopes to 2,000 people. Many of the people who received them were astonished by how accurate and specific the horoscopes were. However, he had actually sent out exactly the same information to everyone. It was the horoscope of a famous criminal.

For the Barnum Effect to work at its best, personality analysis must be complimentary. This is because humans tend to love compliments, but disbelieve criticism. The analysis needn't be entirely positive but any negative comment must be very gentle and possibly be seen as complimentary too.

The Barnum Effect explains the popularity of astrology. Astrological predictions are based on specific information such as the time and place of birth and are nearly always positive. This is especially true of newspaper and magazine horoscopes as they will always try to tell you what you want to hear.

People begin to believe and trust in horoscopes for two reasons. The first is that we like to remember positive or complimentary statements about ourselves. Statements such as 'like most Virgos, you are particularly honest' are typical. After reading a statement like this you may remember an occasion when you were particularly honest and agree that the statement is true. You may even change your behaviour slightly and become more honest as a result.

So remember, we mustn't believe everything we read about ourselves, even if it is complimentary.

Glossary

Barnum Effect: *a psychological theory named after Phineas T Barnum, an American circus owner*

Reading 📼

2 Read the text and complete the summary sentences in your own words.

The Barnum Effect is (1) _____
The Effect works best/well when (2) _____ and
(3) _____
Other reasons astrology is popular are:
People remember (4) _____
People begin to behave (5) _____ the horoscope predicts.

3 What do you think about the arguments you have read? Can you think of any other reasons why astrology is popular?

Vocabulary

4 Find words in the text which mean:

1 section of society (b...)
2 ask for advice or information (c...)
3 positive, flattering (c...)
4 particular, not general (s...)
5 very surprised (a...)
6 a statement about what is going to happen in future (p...)

Improve your grammar

must, mustn't, needn't, have to, don't have to

Look at these examples and answer the questions.
a Feedback *must be* favourable.
b It *need not be* entirely positive.
c An accurate horoscope *needs to be* drawn up.
d We *mustn't* believe everything that we read.
e People *have to* pay for the services of astrologers.

1 Which sentences mean that something is necessary?
2 Which sentence means that something is not necessary?
3 Which sentence means that it is necessary that you do <u>not do</u> something?

Practice

5 Complete the sentences with *must, mustn't,* and *needn't.*

1 To complete your horoscope I _____ have your exact time of birth.
2 You _____ read it if you don't want to, but I hope you will.
3 I want to read my stars. I _____ forget to buy a newspaper.
4 His predictions are usually very accurate. You _____ believe him.
5 According to my horoscope my ideal partner _____ be rich, that's not important, but he _____ be intelligent.
6 You _____ tell me. I've already heard.
7 You _____ tell me. I've been waiting to hear all day.
8 You _____ take astrology seriously. It's a load of rubbish.

6 Rewrite these sentences using *must, mustn't don't have to,* and *needn't.*

Example
You are not allowed to stop here.
You mustn't stop here.

1 Don't go if you don't want to.
2 Don't smoke in class.
3 Tidy up your room before going out.
4 You can come too if you want.
5 Don't tell anyone.
6 It's essential that you buy the book.
7 It isn't necessary for you to be here.

Talking point

7 Read the text about graphology and find out what your handwriting style reveals about your personality. Is it accurate?

Graphology
Graphology tries to explain personality by looking at the size and shape of handwriting. For example, how the letters are joined, dotting of i's and crossing of t's, etc. Although there is no scientific support for graphology, it is very popular, and some employers are using it to select employees.

Slopes
An extreme forward slope indicates an ambitious nature. Backward slopes indicate shyness.

Loops
Large loops below the line express an interest in food, money, possessions, etc. Large loops above the line express an interest in moral values, religion, etc.

The letter T
Long T bars indicate leadership, short T bars that you like to be led.

forward

backward

they

they

twin

twin

8 Do you think your handwriting mirrors your personality? What are the arguments for and against using graphology or astrology to select people for a job? Share your opinions in a small group.

A gap year

Reading 📟

1 Read the text and answer these questions.

1 What is a gap year?
2 Is the writer for or against gap years? Give reasons for your answers.
3 Which one of the options mentioned appeals to you most? Why?

Vocabulary

2 Find words or phrases in the text which mean:

1 the ability to do things without being told what to do (i...)
2 alone, without other people (s...)
3 naturally and without thinking (i...)
4 he did not move (s... s...)
5 made responsible for (p... i... c...)
6 immediately and without delay (p...)
7 a series of connected people (c...)
8 travel from place to place without a plan (d...)
9 stomach troubles (t... u...)

Into the gap

An increasing number of school-leavers in Britain take a gap year between school and university. For young people this is an opportunity for adventure, challenge, and travel. It is also a chance to develop confidence, maturity, and initiative. A gap year can take many forms.

Simon Hepner went on a solo expedition across Africa and was walking along a dirt road when an elephant burst out of the bush and charged. Instinctively, the 19-year-old stayed absolutely still. This must have been the right thing to do because the elephant halted in a cloud of dust.

Alice Elison, 18, worked in a shelter for the homeless in Washington DC, USA. One morning Alice was put in charge of making the evening meal for 1,400 people.

Rachel Kundra went to teach in Mexico to find that her schoolroom was nothing more than a pile of bricks. The 18-year-old Londoner promptly organized a construction programme. Hour after hour in the heat, she stood in a chain of mothers and children, passing bricks to the fathers, who built her schoolroom.

Gap-year adventurers arrive at college wiser and more positive. They go to university with the ability to be independent and live on a tight budget away from home.

A gap year must be carefully planned. It is very easy to waste the year and drift through it delaying tough decisions about the future.

Fortunately, there are numerous organizations helping school-leavers to make good use of their gap year. These organizations help young people find work and adventure abroad. They offer a range of jobs from teaching in Nepal to working on an Australian sheep station.

There are dangers but despite tummy upsets, homesickness, loneliness, and anxious moments, the gap year is a character-shaping experience.

Glossary

living on a tight budget: *living on a small amount of money*

Listening 📼

3 *New Streetwise* asked three readers what they would do in a gap year. Listen and match the speakers to their plans. There is one extra one.

Simon ...	Wants to do something to help the poor.
Alice ...	Wants to start his university course.
Alex ...	Wants to spend a year working in a company.
	Wants to travel.

4 Listen again. Who wants to ...

1 teach English? 2 go to India? 3 be a doctor?

5 Which speaker are you most sympathetic to? Why? Do you think young people should work abroad? Why/Why not?

Improve your grammar

would rather + infinitive or simple past

a *would rather* + infinitive expresses our personal preference for ourselves
Examples
We would rather stay in Britain.
I would rather get on with my course.

b or someone else's personal preference for themselves.
Example
He would rather eat chicken than beef.

c *would rather* can also be used to express what we want someone else to do. In this case *would rather* is followed by a simple past verb (but with a present or future meaning).
Examples
I would rather you stayed here.
My parents would rather I went somewhere in Europe ...

It's time + simple past

d When we want to say that 'it's time' for ourselves or somebody else to do something, we often use the structure *It's time* + subject + past tense verb (with a present or future meaning).
Example
It's time we did something for poorer countries ...

e *It's time* can also be followed by a base form with *to*. This has a similar present/future meaning to *It's time we left*.
Example
It's time to go.

Practice

6 Complete these sentences with an appropriate verb.

1 My parents would rather I ____ at home.
2 We would rather ____ to the United States.
3 He has just joined the army. His parents would rather he ____ a job in a bank.
4 He would rather ____ tea than coffee.

7 Write a sentence with *I'd/We'd rather ...* or *It's time ...* for each situation.

1 Your teacher suggests that you spend a year learning German. You would like to go to China.
2 You want to spend a year on an expedition to the Amazon. Your parents suggest that you work in your father's law firm.
3 A friend has a place in two universities. One is to study engineering. The other is to study medicine. Term starts next week.
4 You are offered a part-time job in a library or a record shop. What is your choice?
5 You are offered a place on a year-long expedition to the South Pole or the Sahara Desert. What would your parents say?
6 You are a brilliant maths student. You want to spend a gap year working in a hospital. What would your teacher say?

Getting Streetwise! 📼

Advice

8 Listen to this conversation and answer the questions.

1 What does the first speaker want to know?
2 What expressions does she use to give advice?
3 How does her friend respond?

Listen and repeat with the same intonation.

9 Imagine that you are the people in the cartoon. Develop a conversation in which you reject your friend's advice. Use as many expressions for giving and responding to advice as you can.

Have you ever thought about leaving school and trying to become a rock star?

Pop music

Warm-up

1 What kind of pop music do you like? Do you prefer foreign pop music or music from your own country?

Reading 🔊

2 Read these extracts from a report on pop music and match them with the headings.

Pop music and fashion	Title
Introduction	The American influence
Conclusion	Pop music and language

(1)_____

> Has pop music changed society?

(2)_____

> The aim of this report is to show the different ways in which pop music has changed society. By looking at fashion, language, and foreign influences we can see the ways that pop music has been an important part of twentieth century life.

(3)_____

> Pop music has made long hair for boys and mini skirts for girls fashionable. Pop music has definitely changed the way we dress. For example, green hair, body piercing, shaved heads, and leather clothes.

(4)_____

> Pop music started in America with Rock and Roll. When Rock and Roll came to Britain it brought with it American cars, food, and style. Since Rock and Roll, Britain has been influenced by America.

(5)_____

> A recent Oxford dictionary includes song lyrics by the Beatles such as *All you need is love* and *Give peace a chance*. Pop music is such an important part of society that it has even influenced our language.

(6)_____

> In conclusion, pop music has had a major influence on life in Britain.

Improve your writing

Writing a report

a Give your report a suitable title.
Example
Pop music today

b Start with an introductory paragraph in which you tell the reader what your report is about.
Example
Introduction
This report is about the different kinds of pop music in my country.

c Make sure the layout of your report is clear. Divide the information in your report into paragraphs and give each paragraph a suitable subheading. These subheadings should help the reader understand the information in the paragraph.
Example
What teenagers like listening to

d Make sure your style is informative and factual. Don't be informal. When writing the report you should try to explain how you got some of your information.
Example
An article in Teen Music magazine said...
This week's MTV pop chart shows how popular girl bands are ...

e Use the information in the report to come to a conclusion about the subject in the final paragraph. Try not to show strong personal opinion.
Example
So, although foreign music is very popular with teenagers, our country's music is ...

4 Do pop musicians in your country use different instruments or equipment? What are they called in English?

Practice

5 Think of a suitable heading for this paragraph from a report about pop music

African, Latin American, and Irish folk music are some of the different types of music from around the world that are becoming increasingly popular.

6 Which of these phrases can you find in the reading text? Which would you use in the introduction and which in the conclusion of a report?

the aim of this report   in conclusion
to sum up   the purpose of this report

Talking point

7 Work in small groups and discuss these questions.

1 What is pop music like in your country?
2 Who are the most popular artists and bands? What kind of music do they play?
3 What instruments do they use? What kind of image do they have?

Writing

8 Follow the *Improve your writing* guidelines and write a report about pop music in your country.

Vocabulary

3 Match the names to the instruments and equipment.

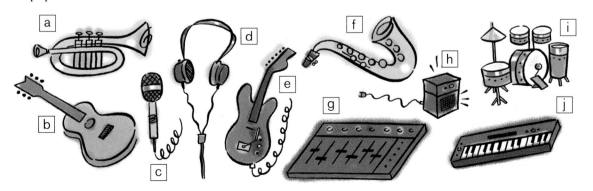

saxophone   electric guitar   acoustic guitar   keyboard   amplifier   microphone   drum kit
trumpet   headphones   mixing desks

Grammar review

Issues 9 and 10

Third conditional

Form

If + past perfect + *would have* + past participle short form: *'d*
(= *had/would*)

Uses	Examples
1 To talk about an event that did not happen because of the condition in the *if* clause. The third conditional is often used for excuses.	*If I had gone, the other man would have taken the picture.* (I didn't go, so I took the picture and the other man didn't.) *If I'd had the money, I would have given them some.* (I didn't, so I didn't give them any.)
2 To talk about a condition that is unreal because it did not and could not happen.	*If I had been born a hundred years ago, I would have had a different life.*

Note
The *if* clause can appear in the second part of the sentence. No comma is used.
I wouldn't have come if I'd known you were busy.

Third conditional with present outcome

Form

If clause	main clause
Imagined condition	Present outcome
past perfect	*would* + infinitive

Example
If Shirley had worn a helmet, she wouldn't have problems with her sight now. (But she didn't, so she has.)

Use	Example
To talk about the present result of an imagined past action.	*If I had worked hard in school, I wouldn't be unemployed.* (But I didn't, so I am.)

Wish/if only + past perfect

Wish or *If only* + past perfect express regret for something that did or didn't happen in the past.
> *I wish I had learned to play the guitar.* (... but I didn't learn to play it.)
> *If only I hadn't failed my exam.* (... but I failed it.)

Note
We can't use *would have* for past regrets.
I wish you had told me. (**Not** ~~I wish you would have told me.~~)

Must, need, have to

Uses	Examples
1 Use both *must* and *have to* to express obligation or necessity.	*I must go, my father is waiting.* *I have to be home by ten.*
2 Use *needn't, don't need to, haven't got to,* or *don't have to* + infinitive to say that it is not necessary to do something.	*I don't need to go to school tomorrow, it's Sunday.* *I haven't got to go to school tomorrow, ...* *I don't have to go ...*
3 Use *mustn't* when there is an obligation not to do something.	*You mustn't sit here.* (= Do not sit here.)

Would rather

1 *Would rather* + infinitive expresses our personal preference for ourselves.

I would rather get on with my course.
We would rather stay in Britain.
He would rather have chicken.

2 *Would rather* can also express what we want someone else to do. In this case it is followed by a verb in the simple past (with a present or future meaning).

My parents would rather I went to India.
I would rather you stayed here.

It's time + simple past

When we want to say that it's time for ourselves or somebody else to do something, we often use the structure *It's time* + subject + simple past (with a present or future meaning).
It's time we did something for poorer countries.
It's time you started revising for the exam.

Note
It's time can also be followed by the infinitive with *to*.
It's time to go is similar to *It's time we left.*

Grammar practice

A ....

1 Put the verb in brackets in an appropriate form.

Example
I wouldn't have done (do) it if I had known.

1 She wouldn't have known if you _____ (not tell) her.
2 We _____ (win) the match if you had played better.
3 Would you have helped if you _____ (be) him?
4 I enjoyed the party but I _____ (not go) if you hadn't asked me.
5 They _____ (arrive) earlier if they hadn't missed the bus.
6 I would have come to see you if I _____ (not leave) your address at home.
7 My mother _____ (not buy) me the shoes even if she had had the money. She really didn't like them.

2 Put in *must, mustn't,* or *needn't.*

1 I'm sorry I can't speak to you now. I _____ finish my homework.
2 The president has given everyone a special holiday, so we _____ go to work tomorrow.
3 I was late for school yesterday. I _____ be late again today.
4 The library has asked me for the books I borrowed. I _____ return them.
5 You _____ buy her a gift for her birthday. She isn't expecting one from you.
6 When I was young I was told that I _____ play with matches.
7 The film was great! You _____ go and see it.

B ....

1 Read each situation and write a sentence with *if.*

Example
She didn't go because she was ill.
If she hadn't been ill, she would have gone.

1 I didn't speak to her because I didn't see her.
2 He didn't buy the book because it was very expensive.
3 She wasn't injured because she wore a helmet.
4 The plants died because he didn't water them.
5 I didn't watch the film because I didn't know it was on.
6 They got lost because the weather was bad.

2 Read each situation and write a sentence with *if,* using the third conditional with a present result.

Example
She is ill because she ate too much.
If she hadn't eaten too much she wouldn't be ill.

1 She is in hospital because she fell off a horse.
2 He is at medical school because he passed all his exams.
3 My uncle speaks fluent French because he learnt it as a child.
4 She is alive because the doctors were able to help her.
5 He lives in Australia because his parents moved there when he was a young boy.
6 He is a lot thinner because he has been on a diet.

3 Finish the sentences so that they mean the same as the sentence before. Use *must, mustn't,* and *needn't.*

1 It is not necessary for me to go to school tomorrow because it is a holiday.
   I _____ .
2 It is essential to stop when you see this sign.
   You _____ .
3 Smoking is forbidden here.
   You _____ .
4 It is very important to study before important exams.
   You _____ .
5 I don't have to change buses to get to his house.
   I _____ .
6 Playing loud music in public is against the law in the UK.
   In the UK, you _____ .

4 Put the verbs in an appropriate form.

Example
I would rather you *went* (go) instead of me.

1 I'd rather you _____ (stay) here.
2 We needn't _____ (hurry). The bus doesn't leave yet.
3 I would rather they _____ (tell) me about it.
4 I wish you _____ (stop) chewing your nails.
5 We'd better _____ (discuss) this another time.
6 It's time we _____ (finish) this exercise.

5 Complete the sentences using an appropriate verb in the past perfect.

remember   buy   eat   wear   study

1 I feel ill. If only _____ .
2 My girlfriend is furious with me because I forgot her birthday. I wish _____ .
3 She got badly sunburnt at the beach. She wishes _____ .
4 He failed his exams, so now he wishes _____ .
5 Those computers were very cheap and now they're expensive. I wish _____ .

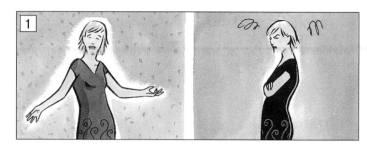

6 Use the pictures to help you to complete the sentences.

Example
1 I would rather *wear red than black.*
2 I would rather _____ .
3 My parents would rather I _____ .
4 I'd rather _____ .
5 The sports teacher would rather you _____ .
6 I would rather _____ .

C ....

1 Complete these sentences to show how life would have been different if you had been born as a member of the opposite sex.
If I had been born a ...   I wouldn't be ...
My parents would have ...   I would have ...
My name ...   I wouldn't have ...

2 Use *I wish* or *If only* + past perfect to list six things that you regret about your life to date.

3 Imagine that some friends are coming to visit you this winter. This is part of their letter.

> 'What clothes should we bring? Do we need an overcoat? What about an umbrella? Is there anything else you would like us to bring?'

Use *must*, *mustn't*, and *needn't* to write a paragraph replying to their question.

Romance

Why do dates with strangers rarely work?

The right to fight

What do you think of people who fight?

True stories

What do you think has happened in this picture?

Romance

Warm-up

1 Discuss your answers to these questions.

1 Where would you go if you went out on a first date with someone of the opposite sex?
2 Who would probably pay for what? Why?

Reading 📼

2 Read this story about a blind date. As you read, decide what went wrong at each stage.

3 Sam and Susan do not want to see each other again. Why? Use your own words to describe the reasons from Sam's and Susan's own points of view.

A Blind Date

The phone call

HER STORY
Sam got my name from a friend. He rang me and invited me to see a film. I accepted, but though I explained that it was time for my piano practice, he started talking about himself, and there was no stopping him. I couldn't have said anything even if I had wanted to!

HIS STORY
Susan is a friend of George. He told me that she had a lovely personality and was really pretty, so I rang her and asked her for a date. I was delighted when she agreed but it was really difficult talking to her. She wouldn't say a word. I had to carry on the whole conversation myself.

The arrival

HER STORY
When he came to pick me up, I was getting ready. When I came to the door and saw the ridiculous outfit he was wearing, I almost died of embarrassment. Then he suggested that we took a bus. I didn't know where to look.

HIS STORY
I got there on time. Her mum answered the door and asked me what I wanted. I explained that I was Susan's date. I think she was impressed by my clothes, and you should have seen Susan's face when she came to the door! As we walked to the bus stop she grumbled that Damian always took her out by car. I told her that she looked lovely!

The film

HER STORY
He laughed so loudly that everybody turned round to look at us. I whispered 'Be quiet' several times but it had no effect. He also made a loud noise eating his popcorn. I was so embarrassed.

HIS STORY
She was a real bore. The film was very funny, but she kept muttering throughout. She refused everything that I offered her.

The meal

HER STORY
He took me to a fast food restaurant, and insisted on ordering a whole meal for me. It was awful. I wasn't even hungry.

HIS STORY
She let me order an extra large meal and she didn't even touch it. She explained that she was still full from lunch, but I think she wanted to go somewhere more expensive. She's a real snob.

The future

HER STORY
Would I go out with him again? You must be joking. I never want to see him again. He was so insensitive.

HIS STORY
I would never call her again. She behaved terribly, and never apologized. One date with her was more than enough.

Glossary

blind date: *a date is an appointment to go out with a member of the opposite sex. A blind date is when you have never met the other person before.*

Talking point

4 Work in small groups. How do you think the date could have gone better? What could each of them have done?

Vocabulary

5 What is the meaning of the expressions in **bold**?

1 saw the **ridiculous outfit** he was wearing
  a fashionable clothes
  b inappropriate clothes that look silly
2 she **was impressed** by my clothes
  a she was shocked by my clothes
  b she admired my clothes
3 she **grumbled** that Damian always took her out by car
  a complained in a bad-tempered way
  b spoke softly
4 I **whispered** 'Be quiet'
  a said something very quietly using only breath
  b shouted
5 she kept **muttering**
  a smiling and being cheerful
  b complaining quietly
6 a real **snob**
  a a person who thinks they are superior
  b a person who dislikes people who are different from them
7 He was so **insensitive**
  a lacking in reason and good sense
  b unaware of other people's feelings

Improve your grammar

Reported speech

a *She explained that she was still full from lunch.*
What were the original words? What did she actually say?
What happens to tenses in reported speech?

b *Would you like to go to a film?*
What time shall we meet?
Decide how you would report these questions if you wanted to report the original words.

c Sometimes we use a verb to give us an idea of what was said, but don't report the exact words.
Example
He telephoned and invited me to see a film, I accepted, and *He started talking about himself.*
How many other examples can you find?

Practice

6 Rewrite these sentences so that you keep the same meaning.

1 'Why do we have to go by bus?'
  She complained about _____ .
2 'Would you like to go to a film?'
  He invited _____ .
3 'Waiter! Two coffees, please.'
  She ordered _____ .
4 'I don't want one.'
  I said _____ .
5 'I'm not hungry.'
  She said _____ .

7 Use these verbs to retell the conversations in reported speech.

offer   insist   apologize   explain   complain
accept   agree   suggest

Harriet	Do you want a coffee?
Sarah	Yes, please.
Harriet	Here you are.
Sarah	It's cold!
Harriet	I'm sorry. Shall I make you another one?
Sarah	Yes, please.
Andy	How about going to the cinema?
Pete	I can't. I've got a lot of homework.
Andy	Oh, come on! Of course you can.
Pete	All right, I'll come with you.

Pronunciation 📼

Tone of voice

8 When we are writing we often use verbs like *whisper, moan, mumble,* etc. to give an idea of how something was said. Work in pairs and decide how you would read these sentences.

1 'Be quiet!' she whispered.
2 'No!' he bellowed.
3 'Ssh,' she said softly.
4 'I don't like it here,' he moaned.
5 'Don't be silly!' she laughed.

Now listen to the tape and repeat the sentences in the same way.

The right to fight

Warm-up

1 Do you think sports like kick-boxing are suitable for both men and women? Why/Why not?

Listening 📼

2 Lisa Shaw is a London business woman. She has a successful business, a young family, and a degree from Oxford University. She also kick-boxes for fun and often takes part in tournaments. Lisa talked to *New Streetwise* about why she kick-boxes. Try and predict her answers before listening to the interview.

1 Lisa kick-boxes because:
   a she is a powerful businesswoman.
   b she has nothing left to achieve.
   c you can't hide behind anything.
   d it teaches her about people.
2 Lisa started kick-boxing:
   a for charity.
   b to make money.
   c to become fit.
   d to learn about herself.
3 Lisa's son:
   a approves of kick-boxing.
   b goes to his mother's fights.
   c broke his nose in training.
   d disapproves of boxing.
4 Lisa's son made a pile of the boxing clothes because:
   a Lisa had decided to quit.
   b Lisa was finished.
   c he wanted Lisa to stop.
   d he was feeling miserable.

Vocabulary

3 Match the words to the definitions.
   pile   degree   charity   quit   tournament
   prejudice

1 stop doing something, give up
2 opinion that is not founded on experience or reason
3 competition in several parts. The winner in one part continues to play in another and at the end there is only one winner
4 giving food, money, or help to those who need it
5 a lot of things on top of one another
6 a qualification you get from a college or university

Improve your grammar

Gerund and infinitive

a If we want to follow *refuse* with a verb, the second verb must be an infinitive (infinitive + *to*).
Example
He refuses to come to any of my fights.

b If we want to follow *enjoy* with a verb, the second verb must be a gerund (-*ing* form).
Example
Lisa Shaw enjoys fighting ...

c Verbs such as *start, begin, continue, intend* can take either an -*ing* form or infinitive + *to* with no difference in meaning:
Example
People started to leave (or started leaving) before the disco was over.

d However, we do not usually have two -*ing* forms together.
It was starting to rain.
Not ~~It was starting raining~~.
Some verbs such as *stop, remember, try, go on*, take -*ing* or an infinitive + *to* with a change of meaning,
What is the difference in meaning between these examples?
1 Although her family didn't like it, she went on fighting.
2 She began by boxing for fun but then she went on to fight in tournaments.

Practice

4 Complete the sentences putting the verb in brackets into either the gerund or the infinitive with *to*.

1 Lisa refuses _____ (give up) kick boxing.
2 Do you enjoy _____ (fight)?
3 Lisa hopes _____ (continue) as a kick boxer.
4 I finished _____ (train) last week.
5 He gave up _____ (box) years ago.
6 Do you ever feel like _____ (go) to fights?
7 I offered _____ (help) him.
8 I forgot _____ (visit) him before I went home.
9 After he had left school he went on _____ (train) as a teacher.

5 Write each pair of sentences as one. Use the *-ing* form or *to* + infinitive.

Example
It was time to have coffee. So the workers stopped.
The workers stopped to have coffee.

1 He had been training for hours. But he went on.
He _____ .
2 He didn't want to go to the gym any more. So he stopped.
He _____ .
3 He wanted to post a letter. He stopped on the way home.
He _____ .
4 Alice didn't bring her text book. She forgot.
Alice _____ .
5 He wanted to try and get fit. He went to the gym.
He tried _____ .
6 I visited Disneyland when I was twelve. I'll never forget it.
I'll never _____ .

Getting streetwise! 📼

Predictions

6 We asked the *New Streetwise* panel if they thought boxing would ever disappear. Listen and find out who used which expression.

Names	Expressions
Mike	I think it's bound to be ...
Alex	I'm sure it would ...
Sandra	I think it's unlikely ...
Alan	I wouldn't be surprised if ...

7 Listen to the tape again. This time, summarize the views of each panel member.

	Predicts	Reason
Mike		
Alex		
Sandra		
Alan		

8 Which panel member do you agree with most? Why?

9 Use these expressions to write your predictions on the future of these sports in your country in the next twenty years.

boxing   golf   tennis   basketball
American football

Example
I bet that American football will become more popular.

True stories

Reading 🔊

1 Read the text and put in the missing expressions.

the daughter said,   'It doesn't matter'
Her father laughed.   Then she said
said her father
the father said apologetically.

The host poured tea into the cups and placed them on the small table in front of his guests. Then he hurried into the kitchen, leaving the teapot on the table.

The guests remained in the sitting room, the ten-year-old daughter looking at the flowers outside the window, her father about to drink his tea, when there was a crash, right there in the sitting room. Something was hopelessly broken.

The teapot had fallen to the floor. The girl looked over her shoulder abruptly, startled, staring. It was mysterious. Neither of them had touched it.

The crash caused the host to rush back from the kitchen with a bowl of sugar in his hand.

'I'm sorry, I touched it and it fell,' (1) _____

(2) _____ , said their host quickly.

Later, when they left the house, (3) _____

'Daddy, did you touch it?'

'No. But it was very close to me.'

'But you didn't touch it. I saw your reflection in the window-pane. You were sitting very still.'

(4) _____ . 'Well how did it fall then?'

'The teapot fell by itself. The floor is uneven. The table wasn't steady. Why did you say that you …'

'It sounds more acceptable when I say I knocked it over. There are things which people believe less the more you explain them. Sometimes, the truer the story you tell, the less true it sounds.'

The daughter was lost in silence for a while.

(5) _____ , 'Can you explain it only this way?'

'Only this way,' (6) _____ .

2 Now answer these questions.

1 Do we know how and why the teapot fell to the ground?
2 Do you think the father did the right thing? What would you have done and said?
3 Do you agree with the statement 'the truer the story you tell, the less true it sounds'? Can you give any examples of true stories which were not believed, or times when it has been easier not to tell the truth?

Improve your writing

Direct and indirect speech in narrative

a Lively narrative often contains a mixture of direct and indirect speech. If you are using direct speech remember the punctuation rules:

- each piece of speech is enclosed by inverted commas.
- every new piece of speech must begin with a capital letter.
- each piece of speech must end with a full stop or an exclamation mark or a question mark before the concluding inverted commas. If the sentence is going to continue, it ends with a comma. This comma also comes before the concluding inverted commas.
- when a piece of speech comes in the middle of a sentence, it must have a comma (or sometimes a colon) just before the opening inverted commas.
- start a new line for each speaker.

b When we use indirect speech in normal speech or when we write a story we often summarize the main points of a conversation.
Example
She suggested that we went out together.

c Look back at the text and find examples of each of these rules.

d We use adverbs of manner such as *gently, slowly, happily* to build up a picture of what happened and to make a story more interesting to read. What adverbs can you find in the text?

Vocabulary

3 Look back at the text. Find where *laughed* and *answered* are used as alternatives to *said*. Try and think of other alternatives to *said*. Combine your list with your partner and try to think of some more. Share your list with the class.

4 Find words in the text that begin with the letters in brackets and mean:

1 quickly (a...)
2 irregular (u...)
3 moved quickly (h...)
4 mirror image (r...)
5 glass in the window (w...-p...)

5 Complete these sentences with adverbs from the list.

rudely   sadly   quickly   doubtfully
naughtily

1 'I'm never going to see you again,' he said
_____ .
2 'Oh shut up,' she said _____ .
3 'Do you think so?' he asked _____ .
4 'I'm not going to do my homework ever again,'
he said _____ .
5 'Stop that!' the teacher said _____ .

Practice

6 Write the sentences putting in the right punctuation.

1 mum ive seen a ghost phillip said
2 his mum smiled and told him not to be silly
3 im not being silly phillip exclaimed i really did see a ghost
4 where did you see a ghost mum asked
5 while I was walking the dog he explained one moment there was a woman in front of me the next moment she wasnt there
6 stop speaking such nonsense mum shouted
7 you never believe me when I tell you the truth do you sighed philip

7 Rewrite this text with a mixture of narrative and direct speech. Remember to use the correct punctuation and layout.

Alan came into the room. His face was white. I asked him what had happened. He just pointed at the ruined building. Later, when he had calmed down, he told me that he had been there alone and the lift had suddenly begun to go up. There hadn't been any sound and it was very strange. I told him he was being silly and laughed at him. I felt strange when Alan quietly said that there was no way the lift could have been moved mechanically. There was no power or electricity and the brake was on.

Writing

8 Imagine you were the daughter in the story and write the story of your father and the teapot. Follow the *Improve your writing* guidelines and use a mixture of direct and indirect speech.

1 Start by describing the incident and where it happened.
2 Talk about the initial reaction of the people there.
3 Highlight your confusion, your father's explanation, and what it has meant for you since then.
4 Begin '*When I was ten I remember ...*'

Self check

9 Re-read your story and make sure that you have followed the punctuation rules for direct and indirect speech. How many adverbs did you use?

New Streetwise songbook

Because you loved me

For all those times that you stood by me,
For all the truth (1) _____,
For all the joy you brought to my life,
For all the wrong (2) _____,
For every dream (3) _____,
For all the love I found in you,
I'll be forever thankfull baby,
You're the one (4) _____,
Never let me fall,
You're the one who saw me through,
Through it all.

You were my strength when I was weak,
You were my voice (5) _____,
You were my eyes (6) _____,
You saw the best there was in me,
Lifted me up (7) _____,
Gave me faith because you believed,
I'm everything I am because you loved me.

You gave me wings and (8) _____,
You touched my hand and I would touch the sky,
I lost my faith you gave it back to me,
You stood by me and I stood tall,
I had your love, I had it all.

1 Look at the song and insert these missing phrases.

made me fly	that you made me see
when I could speak	who helped me up
that you made right	when I couldn't see
you made come true	when I couldn't reach

2 Listen and check your answers.

3 What do you think of the sentiments behind the song? Make a list of what you should expect from someone who loves you. Did your list include things like money? Why/Why not?

Inventors — Who invented these things?

Television

Do you like television? How much television do you watch?

Your area — What do you think of the place where you live?

Inventors

Reading 📼

1 Read the article and decide if these statements are true or false. Give reasons for your answers.

1 Peter Greaves wants to become a professional inventor.
2 Peter started to invent things when he went to school.
3 Peter's hero is a famous inventor.
4 Peter likes to find solutions for everyday problems.
5 Peter has invented a dog-walking gadget.
6 Peter has patented a dog-walking gadget.

Vocabulary

2 Find words in the text that mean:

1 strong desire to be successful (a...)
2 natural ability (t...)
3 answer (s...)
4 new idea (i...)
5 success, large amount of money (f...)

He just can't stop inventing

Peter Greaves is 16. His ambition is to become a successful, professional inventor. Peter became interested in inventing when he learnt about famous inventors at school. His hero is Thomas Edison, the man who invented the light bulb. Edison took out his first patent for an invention when he was nineteen. Peter wants to follow in Edison's footsteps.

Peter, who lives near New York, started to invent things when he was three. His first inventions were toys which he made from old clothes.

Peter, whose latest invention is a gadget that helps old people pick up things without bending down, believes that his talent lies in thinking of solutions for everyday problems. For example, the family dog pulled Peter's father off his bike while they were out on a walk together. So Peter invented a gadget which allows you to ride a bike and walk your dog at the same time. When he tried to patent the idea he found that someone else had got there first.

Peter, who won the young inventor of the year competition, believes that if only he could invent something that was fun, fashionable and appealing to young people, he could make his fortune.

Glossary

patent (n): *an official document giving the holder the sole right to make, use or sell an invention and preventing others from imitating it To patent (v) is to obtain such a document*

gadget: *small object that has been invented to do something useful*

Pronunciation 📟

Words ending in -ion

-tion, -sion and *-shion* are all pronounced /ʃən/ in English.

3 Mark the main stress in each of these words.

competition   invention   fashion   exhibition

1 Listen and check your answers. Where does the stress normally occur?
2 Listen and repeat.

Improve your grammar

Relative clauses

a What is the difference between these two relative clauses?
Edison is the man *who invented the light bulb.*
Peter, *who lives near New York*, started to invent things when he was three.

b When do we use *whose*?
Peter, *whose latest invention is a dog-walking gadget*, helps ...

Practice

4 Rewrite the sentences, using a relative clause to include the information in brackets. The extra information may come in the middle or at the end of the sentence. Do not forget to include the appropriate commas.

1 Peter invented the Supersoap. (It is a ball of soap that floats.)
2 The biro or ballpoint-pen was designed for use underwater. (Its inventor was a Hungarian named Biro.)
3 Edison invented the gramophone and the electric light bulb. (He hid himself in a cupboard under the stairs whenever he wanted to solve a problem.)
4 Blaise Pascal invented the calculator. (He lived in 1647.)
5 Charles Babbage is famous for his invention of the first computer. (He also invented a stethoscope.)

5 Use the prompts to write sentences with *who* or *whose*. Make sure that you include commas where these are appropriate.

1 Leonardo Da Vinci be/great inventor/creations include a model of a submarine.
2 People/invent things/be slightly mad.
3 Rubik/best-selling invention be/Cube be also Hungarian.
4 Peter Greaves/hero is Thomas Edison/is a teenage inventor.
5 Inventors/not sell ideas often find it difficult/make a living.

Listening 📟

6 In Britain, there are companies that sell the very newest inventions. *New Streetwise* spoke to the manager of one of these companies about some of the inventions they sell and some they do not. Listen to the interview and complete the table with the information you hear.

product	do they sell them?	why/why not?
car-shaped ____		
spectacles for ____		
luminous ____ collars		
jumping ____		
motor-powered ____		

Talking point

7 Inventions which are fun, fashionable, and appeal to young people make plenty of money. Which of these is the best invention in recent years? Why?
- a game boy
- a portable CD player
- a play station
- roller blades
- a mountain bike

Television

Warm-up

1 The title of the article about television is 'Electronic Wallpaper'. What do you think it is about?

Reading

2 Read the article and put in the missing phrases. There is one extra phrase.

> TV executives claim the research does not
> However, recent research indicates
> In fact, viewers are very active
> It is a common assumption
> This survey has challenged
> These insights come from
> Using video cameras hidden inside televisions

Vocabulary

3 Find words and expressions in the text that mean:

1 watching television with their full attention (g... t... t... s...)
2 advertisements on television (c...)
3 person who watches television (v...)
4 change quickly from one station to another to find something you want to watch (c... h...)

4 Rewrite these informal expressions in plain English.

1 What's on the telly?
2 He was on the box last night.

Electronic wallpaper

Society blames TV for many of its problems. **1**_____ that we are all heavily influenced by TV and that families spend their evenings 'glued' to their sets. **2**_____ that Britain's most popular programmes often play to total indifference and frequently to nobody at all.

3_____ 7,000 hours of videotapes made by cameras hidden in 100 British homes. Analysis of the tapes shows how television is usually switched on, but often ignored. It shows:

- a man walking out of the room during the news, leaving the prime minister to speak to an empty room;
- a man practising his golf swing during an afternoon chat show;
- the most popular soaps playing to nobody;
- a woman cutting her son's hair during a breakfast show;
- a man folding his laundry during a live match;
- a viewer reading a newspaper during a quiz show.

4_____ , Dr Peter Collett was able to see what was going on inside homes across the country. His results show that viewers who are receptive to the messages of the advertisers and programme makers are a minority. 20% of commercials play to empty rooms and 10% are missed as people look at other channels. Half the time, no-one was actually watching the TV set.

5_____ . As the tapes reveal, viewers often engage in some other activity whilst watching TV, pay no attention or just channel hop. People seem to put the TV on for a bit of background noise when they are on their own and then get on with other things. (6)_____ our view of TV as the most important communication system in the twentieth century. Has TV become merely a form of electronic wallpaper?'

5 What would you expect to see in a typical example of one of these types of television programme?

1 a soap
2 a documentary
3 a chat show
4 a situation comedy
5 breakfast TV

Talking point

6 Carry out a class survey to answer these questions:

1 Does Dr Collett's research reflect what people do while they watch television in your country or not?
2 Does what people do while they are watching television depend on the type of programme they are watching or not?

Improve your grammar

Participle clauses

a Participle clauses are mainly used in written English. The clause can be introduced by the -ing form of the verb or the participle with -ed.
Examples
Opening the window, he leant outside.
Bored by the programme, he fell asleep.

b We use participle clauses to describe how or why something happened.
Example
Using video cameras hidden inside the television, Collett was able to …
Accused of dishonesty by the media, the minister decided to resign.

c To replace defining relative clauses.
Example
The pictures show a man who is folding his laundry …
The pictures show a man folding his laundry …
A scientist who is known as 'Superman' …
A scientist known as 'Superman' …

d With link words such as *when, whenever, before, after, while, since.*
Example
Since starting his research …
After saying goodbye, he left.

Practice

7 Rewrite these sentences with an -ing form participle clause. Make any necessary changes.

Example
Since Dr Collett completed his research, he has become quite famous.
Since completing his research, Dr Collett has become quite famous.

1 The programme which is being broadcast is the nine o'clock news.
2 Alexandra pointed at the stranger and said he reminded her of her maths teacher.
3 While Dr Collett's assistant was looking through the research photographs, he saw a picture of his uncle.
4 While he was looking through the videotapes, Dr Collett noticed that many people did not concentrate on the programmes.
5 He forgot about the camera, so he came into the room without his clothes on.
6 The group worked steadily all morning and finished at noon.

Getting Streetwise! 📼

Criticizing

8 What do you think of television? *New Streetwise* discovered that many of its readers are critical about television. Listen to what they said and tick the expressions used.

I've had enough of …
I'm fed up with …
It's all their fault that …
It gets on my nerves.
It's about time …, isn't it?
They could at least have …
You shouldn't …
Why couldn't they …?

Listen again and write down the programmes they complained about.

9 Would you use these expressions to criticize strangers or complain in shops. Why/Why not?

Your area

1 Which of these brief descriptions is closer to the place where you were born? Why?

'Behind the house I lived in as a young child, there was nothing but fields.'
'We lived in a block of apartments overlooking a busy road.'

Reading

2 Read these descriptions of village and city life and complete the list of things the writers complain about.

Village life: having nothing to do
City life: dirt and pollution

Village life

Do you know what it's like to live in a small village surrounded by countryside? Have you ever been woken up by the sound of cows in the field under your bedroom window? When I was a child, I enjoyed playing outside, riding my bike, and buying sweets at the shop. Now I'm older, I'm bored and fed up with having to travel twenty miles to the nearest town just to buy a CD. I can't get around because I don't have a car and there are only two buses a day. There's a derelict farmhouse near my house which looks sad and empty. I'm not sure when the owners left, but it reminds me that I'm living in a place that's dying. More and more families leave and move into the city every year. Our small village primary school which has been there for almost a hundred and fifty years had to close last year. I can't wait to leave.

City life

Have you thought of what it's like living in a place that is so polluted and dirty that you have to wear a mask when you go out on your bicycle? I live in the city, two minutes from an entertainment complex which has two discos, six restaurants, a bowling alley, and a multi-screen cinema with seven screens. However, I never have the money to go and this makes me feel frustrated. Besides, it's not safe to go out at night on your own. A friend was mugged in this area last week and there is so much traffic that you risk your life crossing the road. We go to the countryside for fresh air whenever we can. I would love to move to a smaller town.

Glossary

mugged: *being attacked and having your bag or purse stolen in the street*

derelict: *disused and rundown*

Talking point

3 Read these newspaper headlines. Which do you think is a better place to grow up? List the advantages of growing up in a village or a city. What kind of place would you like to bring your children up in?

> **Country youths go to the city for the good life**
>
> **Life in the country: safe**
>
> *Bored teenagers vandalize housing estate*

Vocabulary

4 Match the names to the photos.

flat/apartment   mansion
cottage   hut   bungalow

5 Which of these adjectives would you apply to these houses/homes?

derelict   luxurious   old-fashioned
high-rise   single-storey

6 In this context, what is the opposite of:

luxurious   old-fashioned   derelict?

Practice

7 Use *where, who, which* to join these sentences.

Example
I lived in a villa. It was old. It was near the beach.
I lived in an old villa which was near the beach.

1 The street was crowded. It was dirty. It was full of traffic.
2 I lived in a house. It was huge. It was very cold in winter.

3 My neighbours lived four kilometres away. They were very nice.
4 The place I grew up in was quiet. It was boring. It was a village.
5 The hospital was very old. It was very beautiful. It was next door to our house.

8 Join each pair of sentences by using a participle clause.

Example
I lived in an old house. It was built of stone.
I lived in an old house, built of stone.

1 They lived in a villa. The villa was painted white to reflect the sun.
2 The flats were very convenient. They were built near a bus stop.
3 He lives in a small flat. He has lived there since he moved to New York.
4 He remembered the house he was born in. He smiled happily.

Improve your writing

Describing places

a Select a viewpoint for your description. Is the description personal? If so, are you talking about the past or the present?
Example
We were living in ... The house was ...
My flat is on the thirteenth floor ...
Or neutral?
Example
Cambridge is an old city ...

b Create the atmosphere by describing some of the things in detail.
Example
There is a derelict farmhouse near my house which looks sad and empty.
It is so polluted that many people wear masks when they are cycling.

c If the description is personal you should include your feeling about the place.
It reminds me of ...
I makes me feel ...
I remember ...

Writing

9 Follow the *Improve your writing* guidelines and write a personal description of the place you live. What do you feel about the place? What are the advantages and disadvantages of living there? Conclude by talking about where you hope to live in future.

Grammar review

Issues 11 and 12

Reported speech

1 Tense changes

When the reporting verb is in the past (*said, told*, etc.), there are usually tense changes in reported speech.

Direct speech	Reported speech
Simple present	Simple past
Present progressive	Past progressive
Present perfect simple	Past perfect simple
Present perfect progressive	Past perfect progressive
Simple past	Past perfect
Will	Would

Examples

'I'm working.'	She said she was working.
'He has seen it already.'	She said he had seen it already.
'Jack will do it.'	She said Jack would do it.

Exceptions

If the verb in direct speech is in the past, we often leave it in the past in reported speech, unless we want to emphasize the fact that one event happened before another.

| *'I left at six.'* | *He said he left at six.* |

We do not usually change a simple present tense if the statement is always true.

| *'The sun rises in the east.'* | *He said that the sun rises in the east.* |

2 No tense changes

There are no tense changes when we report direct speech with a verb in the present (*say, tell*, etc.). We may choose this when we report a conversation that is still going on, e.g. when someone is talking on the phone, when reading a letter to report what it says, when reading instructions and reporting them, and when reporting something a person says all the time.

This postcard is from Steve and Gaby. They say they're having a great time.

'What do the instructions say?' 'They say cut along the dotted line.'

3 Reported questions

The most common verbs for reporting questions are *ask*, *want to know* and *inquire*.

We report *yes/no* questions with *if* or *whether*.

| *Do you like tea?* | *He asked me if I liked tea.* |

When reporting *wh-* questions we use question words.

| *Why do you like tea?* | *He asked me why I liked tea.* |

4 Reporting the gist

Here are some verbs that allow us to report the gist.

accept	grumble	mutter	respond
beg	invite	offer	threaten
complain	moan	promise	warn
deny	mumble	refuse	

It is possible to report a conversation by giving the gist of what was said rather than the exact words.

He invited us to dinner and we accepted.

Gerund and infinitive

1 Some verbs are followed by the *-ing* form. Here are the most common:

admit	can't stand	feel like
appreciate	deny	finish
avoid	dislike	hate
be used to	dread	keep (= continue)
can't help	enjoy	miss

I can't stand seeing people suffer.
He hates getting up early.

2 Some verbs are followed by the infinitive with *to*. Here are some of the most common.

afford	fail	learn	prepare
appear	forget	manage	promise
arrange	happen	mean	refuse
choose	hope	offer	seem
decide	intend	plan	threaten

I offered to help them.
They're preparing to leave.

3 A few verbs take either *-ing* or *to* with a change of meaning.

stop

I stopped going to the gym a few weeks ago. (= I went to the gym until a few weeks ago, then I stopped.)
I stopped to go to the gym on the way home. (= I was on my way home and I stopped in order to visit the gym.)

remember

I remembered going to the party. (= I remember doing this in the past.)
I remembered to go to the party. (= I remembered the invitation and I went to the party.)

try

I tried taking an aspirin. (= I did an experiment.)
I tried to take an aspirin. (= I made an effort.)

go on
After he left school, he went on to study Maths at university. (= one action followed another)
We went on studying after the end of the lesson. (= We continued studying.)

Relative clauses

Defining and non-defining

1 In defining relative clauses we learn which woman, man, car, etc., the speaker is talking about.
I spoke to the man who lives next door.

2 'Non-defining' relative clauses do not tell us which person, thing, etc., the speaker means; these clauses give us extra, but not absolutely necessary information.
I like my Uncle Jim, who owns four dogs.
Johnson, who lives next door, is an inventor.

These are most common in writing.
When we write these we put commas (,) around the relative clause, except when it comes at the end of the sentence.

Participle clauses

Participle clauses are mainly used in written English. The clause can be introduced by the *-ing* form of the verb, or the past participle.
Opening the window, he learnt out and ...
Bored by the film, she fell asleep in the cinema.
Some of the most common uses of participle clauses are as follows:
1 To describe how or why something happened.
Using video cameras hidden inside the TV, Collett was able to ...
Accused of dishonesty by the media, the minister resigned.
2 To replace defining relative clauses.
The pictures show a man who is folding his laundry.
The pictures show a man folding his laundry.
A scientist who is known as 'Superman' ...
A scientist known as 'Superman' ...
3 With certain link words, like *when, whenever, before, after, while, since.*
Since starting his research, Collett has found ...
After saying goodbye, he left.

Grammar practice

A ....

1 Rewrite each of these sentences so that you keep the same meaning. Start with the words given.

1 'Where is the nearest restaurant?' asked the tourist.
The tourist _____ .
2 'Stop and don't go any further,' said the policeman.
The policeman ordered them _____ .
3 Charles said, 'I haven't seen Ann for years.'
Charles told me _____ .
4 Helen told me that she liked him.
Helen said, '_____ .'
5 'Are you alone?' Chris asked.
Chris wanted _____ .
6 'Tom saw me on his way to work,' he said.
He told me _____ .
7 She said she had worked in Australia two years ago.
Margaret said, '_____ .'

2 Join the two sentences using *who, which,* or *whose.* Make any changes that are necessary.

Example
That's Mary. Her sister is my teacher.
That's Mary whose sister is my teacher.

1 That is Alan. I saw him at the match.
2 The Baiji is a dolphin. It lives in the Yangtze.
3 She is the girl. Her walkman was stolen.
4 Do you know that boy? Alan is talking to him.
5 I rented a bike. It was green.
6 Those are the people. Their dog is the same as ours.
7 I spoke to Alice. She is in your class.

3 Put the verbs in brackets into either *-ing* or *to +* infinitive.

1 Did you remember _____ (stop) and buy me a hamburger?
2 I forgot _____ (remind) him.
3 Why don't you try _____ (wear) green socks with that suit?
4 They stopped _____ (go) to violin lessons when they left school.
5 I'm sorry I forgot _____ (bring) your book.
6 I'll remember _____ (send) you a postcard from Germany.
7 First, he had a job in a shop. Then he went on _____ (work) in a garage.
8 I asked him to stop, but he went on _____ (sing).

B ···

1 Complete the sentences with an *-ing* form or participle of the verbs below.

make   walk   do   know   leave   sell   lie   say

1 He is _____ as a hard worker.
2 The painting shows a woman _____ her washing.
3 I gave money to the people _____ homeless by the war.
4 The people _____ to the match were singing.
5 Look at that dog _____ in the middle of the road.
6 He only buys clothes _____ at half price.
7 Since _____ university, he has got himself a good job.
8 He left after _____ hello to a few people.

2 Join each pair of sentences using a present participle.

Example
Who is that man? He is speaking to my sister.
Who is that man speaking to my sister?

1 There is a crowd outside the concert hall. They are waiting to see Jason.
2 My little brother hurt himself. He was trying to climb a high wall.
3 John broke his leg. He was running down the stairs.
4 The dog was crossing the road. It was hit by a car.
5 I arrived home at midnight. I wasn't feeling very well.

3 Finish each of the following sentences in such a way that it means the same as the sentence before it.

1 Did I see him? I don't remember.
  I don't remember _____ .
2 'Let's go waterskiing next week,' said John.
  John suggested _____ .
3 My teacher gets angry when students sleep in class.
  My teacher can't stand _____ .
4 The little boy said that he had hadn't taken the cake.
  The little boy denied _____ .
5 I have enough money to buy a new stereo.
  I can afford _____ .
6 He did not succeed in passing the exam.
  He failed _____ .

4 Use verbs in the list to report what was said in each situation.

warn   invite   deny   accept   threaten   offer   grumble

a Don't be late, or I'll be angry.
b I didn't do it!
c Can you come to my party?
d Yes, I'd love to.
e I'll leave the team!
f We'll give you a new car.
g I have too much homework.

C ···

1 Tell a pen friend about TV in your country. Your letter should answer these questions:

1 What is the most popular programme?
2 Who is the most popular television personality?
3 What is your favourite programme?
4 What is the most boring programme?
5 Which is the most popular soap opera?
6 Which programmes do young people like?

Example
The most popular programme in the UK is Coronation Street, which is a soap opera.

2 This is the last line of a conversation between the people in the picture. Continue this report of the conversation that led up to it.

I promise I won't do it again.

Last night, I was listening to music in my room. Dad came up to my room and …

Wordlist

Issue one
part one

advertising /ˈædvəˌtaɪzɪŋ/
album /ˈælbəm/
banks /bæŋks/
brand conscious /ˈbrænd ˌkɒnʃəs/
cash /kæʃ/
changing room /ˈtʃeɪndʒɪŋ ruːm/
consumer /kənˈsjuːmə(r)/
designer clothes /dɪˌzaɪnə ˈkləʊðz/
exclusive /ɪkˈskluːsɪv/
fashion conscious /ˈfæʃn ˌkɒnʃəs/
impulsive /ˌɪmˈpʌlsɪv/
latest /ˈleɪtɪst/
magazine /ˌmægəˈziːn/
mirror /ˈmɪrə/
music video /ˈmjuːzɪk ˈvɪdiəʊ/
questionnaire /ˌkwestʃəˈneə(r)/
relaxed (adj) /rɪˈlakst/
shopping /ˈʃɒpɪŋ/
slim /slɪm/
spend /spend/
styles /staɪlz/
teenager /ˈtiːneɪdʒə(r)/
typical /ˈtɪpɪkl/
quality /ˈkwɒliti/
wide /waɪd/

Issue one
part two

addict /ˈædɪkt/
baked potato /ˈbeɪkt pəˈteɪtəʊ/
bitter /ˈbɪtə(r)/
calories /ˈkæləriz/
cardboard /ˈkɑːdbɔːd/
chain /tʃeɪn/
chillies /ˈtʃɪliz/
compliment /ˈkɒmplɪmənt/
covered /ˈkʌvəd/
creamy /ˈkriːmi/
delicious /dɪˈlɪʃəs/
diet /ˈdaɪət/
disgusting /dɪsˈɡʌstɪŋ/
disposable /dɪsˈpəʊzəbl/
doughnut /ˈdəʊnʌt/
energy /ˈenədʒi/
fast food /fɑːst ˈfuːd/
fattening /ˈfætnɪŋ/
fries /fraɪz/
healthy /ˈhelθi/
hot /hɒt/
juicy /ˈdʒuːsi/
milkshake /ˈmɪlkʃeɪk/
nasty /ˈnɑːsti/
outfit /ˈaʊtfɪt/
pitta bread /ˈpɪtə ˌbred/
plastic /ˈplæstɪk/

potato crisps /pəˌteɪtəʊ ˈkrɪsps/
rich /rɪtʃ/
salty /ˈsɒlti/
sausage /ˈsɒsɪdʒ/
slice /slaɪs/
spicy /ˈspaɪsi/
superb /suːˈpɜːb/
sweet /swiːt/
tempting /ˈtemtɪŋ/
tomato sauce /təˌmɑːtəʊ ˈsɔːs/
vegetarian /ˌvedʒəˈteəriən/
yoghurt /ˈjɒɡət/

Issue one
part three

cool /kuːl/
exclamation /ˌekskləˈmeɪʃn/
exercise /ˈeksəsaɪz/
gossip /ˈɡɒsɪp/
hang out /hæŋ ˈaʊt/
invitation /ˌɪnvɪˈteɪʃn/
karate /kəˈrɑːti/
presentation /ˌprezənˈteɪʃn/
scary /ˈskeəri/
settled /ˈsetld/
surviving /səˈvaɪvɪŋ/
underlining /ʌndəˈlaɪnɪŋ/
weird /wɪəd/

Songbook

address unknown /əˌdres ʌnˈnəʊn/
fall in love /ˌfɔːl ɪn ˈlʌv/
mailbox /ˈmeɪlbɒks/
postman /ˈpəʊs(t)mən/
quarrel /ˈkwɒrəl/
relationship /rɪˈleɪʃnˌʃɪp/
Return to sender /rɪˌtɜːn tə ˈsendə/
sack (n) /sæk/
zone /zəʊn/

Issue two
part one

adult /ˈædʌlt, əˈdʌlt/
A level English /ˈeɪ levl ˈɪŋglɪʃ/
automatically /ˌɔːtəˈmætɪkli/
behave /bɪˈheɪv/
clap /klæp/
classroom /ˈklɑːsruːm, -rʊm/
cleaning /ˈkliːnɪŋ/
confidence /ˈkɒnfɪdəns/
confident /ˈkɒnfɪdənt/
embarrassed /ɪmˈbærəst/
inhibit /ɪnˈhɪbɪt/
intelligent /ɪnˈtelɪdʒənt/
ironing /ˈaɪənɪŋ/
make a fool of somebody /meɪk ə ˈfuːl əv ˌsʌmbədi/
mature /məˈtʃʊə(r)/

pillow /ˈpɪləʊ/
pour /pɔə(r)/
prediction /prɪˈdɪkʃn/
respect /rɪsˈpekt/
shared /ʃeəd/
study (v) /ˈstʌdi/
surround /sʌˈraʊnd/
term /tɜːm/
time off /taɪm ˈɒf/
traffic jam /ˈtræfɪk ˌdʒæm/
wear off /weər ˈɒf/

Issue two
part two

alcoholic /ˌælkəˈhɒlɪk/
arrest (v) /əˈrest/
calf /kɑːf/
captivity /kæpˈtɪvɪti/
capture /ˈkæptʃə(r)/
curious /ˈkjʊəriəs/
difficult /ˈdɪfɪkəlt/
dolphin /ˈdɒlfɪn/
drift net /ˈdrɪft net/
encourage /ɪnˈkʌrɪdʒ/
expel /ekˈspel/
experience (n) /ɪksˈpɪəriəns/
exploit (v) /ɪksˈplɔɪt/
gentle /ˈdʒentl/
intense /ɪnˈtens/
in the wild /ˌɪn ðə ˈwaɪld/
lagoon /ləˈguːn/
margarine /ˌmɑːdʒəˈriːn/
environment /ɪnˈvaɪrəmənt/
neutral /ˈnjuːtrəl/
rehabilitation /ˌriːhəbɪlɪˈteɪʃn/
scheme /skiːm/
sonar /ˈsəʊnɑː/
supplier /səˈplaɪə/
therapy /ˈθerəpi/
tinned /tɪnd/
treatment /ˈtriːtmənt/
tuna /ˈtjuːnə/
vote (v) /vəʊt/
whale /weɪl/
witness (v) /ˈwɪtnəs/

Issue two
part three

application /æplɪˈkeɪʃn/
caring /ˈkeərɪŋ/
consider /kənˈsɪdə/
details /ˈdiːteɪlz/
discuss /dɪsˈkʌs/
enthusiastic /ɪnˌθjuːziˈæstɪk/
experienced /ɪksˈpɪəriənst/
flexible /ˈfleksɪbl/
hard-working /hɑːd ˈwɜːkɪŋ/
highly-motivated /ˌhaɪli ˈməʊtɪveɪtɪd/
honest /ˈɒnɪst/
inappropriate /ˌɪnəˈprəʊpriət/
musical /ˈmjuːzɪkl/
organize /ˈɔːɡənaɪz/
require /rɪˈkwaɪə/
response /rɪsˈpɒns/
scholarship /ˈskɒləʃɪp/

skill /skɪl/
sociable /ˈsəʊʃəbl/
word processor /ˈwɜːd ˌprəʊsesə/

Issue three
part one

agonizing /ˈægənaɪzɪŋ/
ambulance /ˈæmbjələns/
amusement /əˈmjuːzmənt/
be stranded /bi ˈstrændɪd/
burst into tears /ˌbɜːst ɪntə ˈtɪəz/
cable car /ˈkeɪbl kɑː/
desperately /ˈdesprətli/
emergency services /ɪˌmɜːdʒənsi ˈsɜːvɪsɪz/
equipment /ɪˈkwɪpmənt/
escape /ɪˈskeɪp/
fiancée /fɪˈɒnseɪ/
fireman /ˈfaɪəmən/
halt /hɒlt/
helicopter /ˈhelɪˌkɒptə/
high winds /haɪ ˈwɪndz/
holidaymaker /ˈhɒlɪdeɪ ˌmeɪkə/
injury /ˈɪndʒəri/
ladder /ˈlædə/
lower (v) /ˈləʊə(r)/
magnesium /mægˈniːziəm/
ravine /rəˈviːn/
relieved /rəˈliːvd/
rescue (v) /ˈreskjuː/
rescuer /ˈreskjuːə/
reunite /ˌriːjuːˈnaɪt/
scenery /ˈsiːnəri/
tangled /ˈtæŋgld/
terrified /ˈterɪfaɪd/
terror /ˈterə(r)/
thrill /θrɪl/
trap (v) /træp/
wheelchair /ˈwiːltʃeə(r)/

Issue three
part two

angelic /ænˈdʒelɪk/
be ruined /bi ˈruːɪnd/
bridesmaid /ˈbraɪdzmeɪd/
crawl /krɔːl/
curiosity /kjʊriˈɒsɪti/
deal with /ˈdiəl wɪð/
despair (n) /dɪsˈpeə(r)/
drop out of something /drɒp ˈaʊt əv ˌsʌmθɪŋ/
engineer /endʒɪˈnɪə/
fall out with someone /fɔːl ˈaʊt wɪð ˌsʌmwən/
flood (v) /flʌd/
get away with /get əˈweɪ wɪð/
get on with /get ˈɒn wɪð/
get up to /get ˈʌp tə/
grin /grɪn/
inquisitive /ɪnˈkwɪzətɪv/
kitchen sink /ˌkɪtʃɪn ˈsɪŋk/
let somebody off /ˌlet ˌsʌmbɒdi ˈɒf/
naughty /ˈnɔːti/

oblige someone to do something /əˌblaɪdʒ sʌmwʌn tə ˈduː sʌmθɪŋ/
punish /ˈpʌnɪʃ/
replace /rɪˈpleɪs/
severe /səˈvɪə(r)/
slap /slæp/
strict /strɪkt/
sulk /sʌlk/
wardrobe /ˈwɔːdrəʊb/
washing machine /ˈwɒʃɪŋ məˈʃiːn/

Issue three
part three
accuse /əˈkjuːz/
afraid /əˈfreɪd/
angry /ˈæŋgri/
annoyed /əˈnɔɪd/
ashamed /əˈʃeɪmd/
bored /bɔːd/
boss /bɒs/
dilemma /dɪˈlemə, daɪ-/
disappointed /dɪsəˈpɔɪntɪd/
doubt /daʊt/
dramatic /drəˈmætɪk/
fed up /fed ˈʌp/
fond /fɒnd/
frustrated /frʌsˈtreɪtɪd/
guilty /ˈgɪlti/
increase (v) /ɪnˈkriːs/
interested /ˈɪntrestɪd/
invent /ɪnˈvent/
keen /kiːn/
missing /ˈmɪsɪŋ/
persuade /pəsˈweɪd/
pleased /pliːzd/
pocket money /ˈpɒkɪt ˌmʌni/
responsibility /rɪsˌpɒnsɪˈbɪlɪti/
responsible /rɪsˈpɒnsəbl/
staff /stɑːf/
suspect (v) /səsˈpekt/
suspicious /səsˈpɪʃəs/
tired /ˈtaɪəd/
vacancy /ˈveɪkənsi/
viewpoint /ˈvjuːpɔɪnt/
worried /ˈwɒriːd/

Songbook
confused /kənˈfjuːzd/
get away /get əˈweɪ/
heart /hɑːt/
outer space /aʊtə ˈspeɪs/
lines /laɪnz/

Issue four
part one
access (n) /ˈækses/
access (v) /ˈækses/
age group /ˈeɪdʒ gruːp/
anti-ageing /ˌænti ˈeɪdʒɪŋ/
attach importance to /əˌtætʃ ɪmˈpɔːtns tuː/
carry on /ˈkæri ˈɒn/
deliberate (adj) /dɪˈlɪbərət/
e-mail /ˈiː meɪl/

enjoyable /ɪnˈdʒɔɪəbl/
evidence /ˈevɪdəns/
fad /fæd/
fan /fæn/
finishing line /ˈfɪnɪʃɪŋ ˌlaɪn/
furniture /ˈfɜːnɪtʃə(r)/
goal /gəʊl/
goal line /ˈgəʊl laɪn/
groceries /ˈgrəʊsəriz/
irrelevant /ɪˈrelɪvənt/
keyboard /ˈkiːbɔːd/
look after /lʊk ˈɑːftə/
monitor (n) /ˈmɒnɪtə/
natural resources /ˌnætʃrəl rɪˈzɔːsɪz/
on-line /ɒn ˈlaɪn/
passion /ˈpæʃn/
penalty /ˈpenəlti/
physical /ˈfɪzɪkl/
pitch /pɪtʃ/
popular /ˈpɒpjələ(r)/
pressure pad /ˈpreʃə pæd/
referee /refəˈriː/
research (n) /ˈriːsɜːtʃ/
robot /ˈrəʊbɒt/
select /sɪˈlekt/
solve /sɒlv/
stay in touch /ˌsteɪ ɪn ˈtʌtʃ/
surf (v) /sɜːf/
technology /tekˈnɒlədʒiː/
the net /ðə ˈnet/
transmit /trænsˈmɪt/
video replay /ˌvɪdɪəʊ ˈriːpleɪ/

Issue four
part two
anxiety /aŋˈzaɪəti/
anxious /ˈæŋkʃəs/
appearance /əˈpɪərəns/
arrangement /əˈreɪndʒmənt/
candidate /ˈkændɪdət/
chew /tʃuː/
collected (adj) /kəˈlektɪd/
count for a lot /ˌkaʊnt fər ə ˈlɒt/
CV /siːˈviː/
demand (v) /dɪˈmɑːnd/
dread /dred/
eye contact /ˈaɪ ˈkɒntækt/
fear (n) /fɪə(r)/
flustered /ˈflʌstəd/
get worked up /ˌget wɜːkt ˈʌp/
go blank /ˈgəʊ ˈblæŋk/
grade (n) /greɪd/
highlight /ˈhaɪlaɪt/
impression /ɪmˈpreʃn/
interviewee /ˌɪntəvjuːˈiː/
nervousness /ˈnɜːvəsnəs/
off-putting /ˈɒf pʊtɪŋ/
panel /ˈpænl/
patiently /ˈpeɪʃntli/
performance /pəˈfɔːməns/
pleasantly /ˈplezəntli/
put someone off /ˈpʊt sʌmwʌn ˌɒf/

reception /rəˈsepʃn/
retire /rɪˈtaɪə/
revision /rəˈvɪʒn/
scruffy /ˈskrʌfi/
slouched /ˈslaʊtʃt/
smartly /ˈsmɑːtli/
tip (n) /tɪp/
turn someone down /ˌtɜːn sʌmwʌn ˈdaʊn/
unemotional /ˌʌnɪˈməʊʃənl/
washed and pressed /ˌwɒʃt ənd ˈprest/

Issue four
part three
argument /ˈɑːgjumənt/
charity events /ˌtʃærɪti ɪˈvents/
claim /kleɪm/
community /kəˈmjuːnɪti/
complain /kəmˈpleɪn/
conclusion /kənˈkluːʒn/
conflict (n) /ˈkɒnflɪkt/
contact /ˈkɒntækt/
despite /dɪsˈpaɪt/
facilities /fəˈsɪlətiz/
friction /ˈfrɪkʃn/
generation /ˌdʒenəˈreɪʃn/
moaning /ˈməʊnɪŋ/
privacy /ˈprɪvəsi/
property /ˈprɒpəti/
vandal /ˈvændl/
vandalize /ˈvændəlaɪz/

Issue five
part one
achievement /əˈtʃiːvmənt/
agriculture /ˈægrɪkʌltʃə(r)/
aliens /ˈeɪliːənz/
ancient /ˈeɪntʃənt/
astronaut /ˈæstrənɔːt/
belief /bɪˈliːf/
believable /bɪˈliːvəbl/
blow (n) /bləʊ/
culture /ˈkʌltʃə(r)/
domed /dəʊmd/
effect /ɪˈfekt/
explanation /ˌekspləˈneɪʃn/
flying saucer /ˌflaɪŋ ˈsɔːsə/
forest /ˈfɒrɪst/
galaxy /ˈgæləksi/
hangar /ˈhæŋə/
helmet /ˈhelmɪt/
idea /aɪˈdɪə/
impact (n) /ˈɪmpakt/
in support of /ɪn səˈpɔːt əv/
interpretation /ɪnˌtɜːprɪˈteɪʃn/
investigate /ɪnˈvestɪgeɪt/
kidnap /ˈkɪdnæp/
lie detector /ˈlaɪ dɪˌtektə/
Mesopotamia /ˌmesəpəˈteɪmiə/
mystery /ˈmɪstri/
mythologies /mɪˈθɒlədʒiːz/
observe /əbˈzɜːv/
panic (v) /ˈpænɪk/
phone booth /ˈfəʊn ˈbuːð/
planetarium /plænɪˈteəriəm/

point out /pɔɪnt ˈaʊt/
publish /ˈpʌblɪʃ/
pyramid /ˈpɪrəmɪd/
ranging from /ˈreɪndʒɪŋ frɒm/
reveal /rɪˈviːl/
scholar /ˈskɒlə/
search /sɜːtʃ/
shaky /ˈʃeɪki/
spaceship /ˈspeɪsʃɪp/
statement /ˈsteɪtmənt/
statistics /stəˈtɪstɪks/
theory /ˈθɪəri/
turn up (v) /tɜːn ˈʌp/
UFO /juː ef ˈəʊ/
uniform /ˈjuːnɪfɔːm/
varying between /ˈveəriɪŋ ˌbɪtwiːn/

Issue five
part two
ambidextrous /ˌæmbɪˈdekstrəs/
anti-clockwise /ˌænti ˈklɒkwaɪz/
association /əˌsəʊsiˈeɪʃn/
backwards /ˈbækwədz/
Bill of Rights /ˌbɪl əv ˈraɪts/
custom /ˈkʌstəm/
discriminate /dɪsˈkrɪmɪneɪt/
equally /ˈiːkwəli/
focus /ˈfəʊkəs/
forwards /ˈfɔːwədz/
grab /græb/
ignore /ɪgˈnɔː(r)/
left-handed /left ˈhændɪd/
left-hander /left ˈhændə/
minority /maɪˈnɒrɪti/
opposite /ˈɒpəzɪt/
palindrome /ˈpælɪndrəʊm/
profile /ˈprəʊfaɪl/
provide /prəˈvaɪd/
reservation /ˌrezəˈveɪʃn/
reverse /rɪˈvɜːs/
right-handed /raɪt ˈhændɪd/
right-hander /raɪt ˈhændə/
salute /səˈluːt/
scissors /ˈsɪzəz/
sideways /ˈsaɪdweɪz/
stand over someone /stænd ˈəʊvə ˌsʌmwʌn/
task /tɑːsk/
treat /triːt/
up-to-date /ˌʌp-tə-ˈdeɪt/

Issue five
part three
although /ɔːlˈðəʊ/
amusing /əˈmjuːzɪŋ/
attractive /əˈtræktɪv/
backpacker /ˈbækpækə/
character /ˈkærəktə/
classic /ˈklæsɪk/
costume /ˈkɒstjuːm/
dialogue /ˈdaɪəlɒg/
dramatically /drəˈmætɪkli/
enemy /ˈenəmi/
fictional /ˈfɪkʃənl/
flash (v) /flæʃ/

glamorous /'glæmərəs/
handsome /'hænsəm/
hilarious /hɪ'leərɪəs/
impressive /ɪm'presɪv/
in addition /ɪn ə'dɪʃn/
light-hearted /laɪt 'hɑːtɪd/
masked ball /'mɑːskt bɔːl/
memorable /'memrəbl/
moving /muːvɪŋ/
on location /ɒn ləʊ'keɪʃn/
plot /plɒt/
recommend /ˌrekə'mend/
ridiculous /rɪ'dɪkjələs/
romance /'rəʊmæns/
romantic comedy /rəʊˌmæntɪk
  'kɒmədi/
screen /skriːn/
setting /'setɪŋ/
soundtrack /'saʊndtræk/
special effects /ˌspeʃl ɪ'fekts/
stunning /'stʌnɪŋ/
terrifying /'terɪfaɪɪŋ/
version /'vɜːʒn/

Songbook

break someone's heart /ˌbreɪk
  sʌmwʌnz 'hɑːt/
maturity /mə'tjʊərɪti/
to be through with
  something/someone /tə biː
  'θruː wɪð ˌsʌmwʌn/

Issue six
part one

abolish /ə'bɒlɪʃ/
army /'ɑːmi/
break in /breɪk 'ɪn/
bully (v) /'bʊli/
clear your throat /ˌklɪə jɔː
  'θrəʊt/
conch /kɒntʃ/
copy-cat /'kɒpi kæt/
crazy /'kreɪzi/
disbelief /ˌdɪsbə'liːf/
election /ɪ'lekʃn/
flattering (adj) /'flætərɪŋ/
fluently /'fluːəntli/
gang /gæŋ/
glance /glɑːns/
hesitation /ˌhezɪ'teɪʃn/
hum /hʌm/
hunt (v) /hʌnt/
hunter /'hʌntə/
imitate /'ɪmɪteɪt/
imitator /'ɪmɪteɪtə/
incredible /ɪn'kredɪbl/
inflict /ɪn'flɪkt/
insult (n) /'ɪnsʌlt/
irritating /'ɪrɪ,teɪtɪŋ/
It's pathetic /ɪts pə'θetɪk/
leader /'liːdə/
lightweight /'laɪtweɪt/
lose control /ˌluːz kən'trəʊl/
obey /ə'beɪ/
savage (adj) /'sævɪdʒ/
shelter (n) /ʃeltə(r)/

signal (n) /'sɪgnəl/
tension /'tenʃn/

Issue six
part two

amazing /ə'meɪzɪŋ/
be flattered /biː 'flætəd/
cross (adj) /krɒs/
do away with /duː ə'weɪ wɪð/
drives me crazy /ˌdraɪvz miː
  'kreɪzi/
get out of /get aʊt əv/
get through (something) /get
  'θruː sʌmθɪŋ/
imitation /ɪmɪ'teɪʃn/
keep up with /kiːp 'ʌp wɪð/
peace /piːs/
persecute /'pɜːsɪkjuːt/
praise (v) /preɪz/
pull someone's leg /'pʊl
  sʌmwʌnz 'leg/
rivalry /'raɪvəlri/
rule (n) /ruːl/
shampoo /ʃæm'puː/
short-sighted /ˌʃɔːt 'saɪtɪd/
survive /sɜː'vaɪv/
taste (n) /teɪst/

Issue six
part three

advice /əd'vaɪs/
advise /əd'vaɪz/
audience /'ɔːdɪəns/
chat like mad /ˌtʃæt laɪk 'mæd/
defence /dɪ'fens/
depressed /dɪ'prest/
friendly /'frendli/
get embarrassed /get ɪm'bærəst/
item /'aɪtəm/
moral support /mɒrəl sə'pɔːt/
put someone at their ease /ˌpʊt
  sʌmwʌn æt ðeər 'iːz/
respond /rɪ'spɒnd/
self-confidence /self 'kɒnfɪdəns/
shyness /'ʃaɪnəs/
suit /suːt/
symptom /'sɪmptəm/

Issue seven
part one

adventurous /æd'ventʃərəs/
approve /ə'pruːv/
arranged marriage /ə'reɪndʒd
  'mærɪdʒ/
astrologer /ə'strɒlədʒə(r)/
be suited /biː 'suːtɪd/
bizarre /bɪ'zɑː(r)/
bride /braɪd/
ceremony /'serəməni/
church /tʃɜːtʃ/
commitment /kə'mɪtmənt/
competition /ˌkɒmpə'tɪʃn/
condemn /kən'dem/
convertible /kən'vɜːtəbl/
couple (n) /kʌpl/
divorce rate /dɪ'vɔːs reɪt/

entrant /'entrənt/
Europe /'jʊərəp/
experiment /ɪk'sperɪmənt/
fashion (n) /fæʃn/
finalist /'faɪnəlɪst/
groom (n) /gruːm/
guarantee (v) /ˌgærən'tiː/
honeymoon /'hʌni:muːn/
immoral /ɪ'mɒrəl/
ivory /'aɪvəri/
last (v) /lɑːst/
less than delighted /les ðən
  dɪ'laɪtɪd/
licensed (adj) /'laɪsənst/
live on radio /laɪv ɒn 'reɪdɪəʊ/
luxury apartment /'lʌkʃəri
  ə'pɑːtmənt/
marriage /'mærɪdʒ/
marriage guidance service
  /ˌmærɪdʒ 'gaɪdəns sɜːvɪs/
mosque /mɒsk/
multi-cultural /'mʌlti 'kʌltʃərəl/
option /'ɒpʃn/
personality /pɜːsə'næliti/
photographer /fə'tɒgrəfə(r)/
population /pɒpjə'leɪʃn/
reflect /rɪ'flekt/
registry office /'redʒɪstri 'ɒfɪs/
religious /rə'lɪdʒəs/
saleswoman /'seɪlzwʊmən/
significant /sɪg'nɪfɪkənt/
tense (adj) /tens/
tradition /trə'dɪʃn/
wedding /'wedɪŋ/
wedding breakfast /'wedɪŋ
  ˌbrekfəst/

Issue seven
part two

academic /ˌækə'demɪk/
apparatus /ˌæpə'reɪtəs/
attention /ə'tenʃn/
attitude /'ætɪtjuːd/
be convinced /biː kən'vɪnst/
considerably /kən'sɪdərəbli/
cringe /krɪndʒ/
current trend /ˌkʌrənt 'trend/
dominate /'dɒmɪneɪt/
favour (v) /'feɪvə/
hardly any /ˌhɑːdli 'eni/
loathe (v) /ləʊð/
marginally /'mɑːdʒɪnli/
misbehave /mɪsbɪ'heɪv/
pass rate /'pɑːs reɪt/
single-sex school /ˌsɪŋgl seks
  'skuːl/
slightly /'slaɪtli/
survey (n) /'sɜːveɪ/
unruly /ʌn'ruːli/
unsophisticated
  /ˌʌnsə'fɪstɪkeɪtɪd/

Issue seven
part three

ambitious /æm'bɪʃəs/
aggressive /ə'gresɪv/

assertive /ə'sɜːtɪv/
easy-going /ˌiːzi 'gəʊɪŋ/
filthy /'fɪlθɪ/
frank /fræŋk/
generous /'dʒenərəs/
groan (n) /grəʊn/
gross /grəʊs/
habit /'hæbɪt/
mean /miːn/
moan (n) /məʊn/
mobile phone /məʊbaɪl 'fəʊn/
naff /næf/
pet hate /pet heɪt/
polite /pə'laɪt/
pride /praɪd/
primary school /'praɪməri
  ˌskuːl/
reliable /rɪ'laɪəbl/
rude /ruːd/
scream (v) /skriːm/
secretive /'siːkrətɪv/
sense of humour /ˌsens əv
  'hjuːmə(r)/
sensible /'sensəbl/
sensitive /'sensətɪv/
silly /'sɪli:/
stubborn /'stʌbən/
talkative /'tɔːkətɪv/
tease /tiːz/

Songbook

ache (v) /eɪk/
fall in love /ˌfɔːl ɪn 'lʌv/
let something go /let ˌsʌmθɪŋ
  'gəʊ/

Issue eight
part one

admit to /æd'mɪt tə/
aerosol /'eərəsɒl/
apologize /ə'pɒlədʒaɪz/
be drawn in /biː drɔːn 'ɪn/
call in on /kɔːl 'ɪn ɒn/
come across /ˌkʌm ə'krɒs/
diamond /'daɪmənd/
energetic /enə'dʒetɪk/
get involved /ˌget ɪn'vɒlvd/
get on with someone /get 'ɒn
  wɪð ˌsʌmwʌn/
ingredient /ɪn'griːdɪənt/
let down /let 'daʊn/
look up to /lʊk 'ʌp tə/
own up /əʊn 'ʌp/
pass on /pɑːs 'ɒn/
put up with /pʊt 'ʌp wɪð/
recipe /'resɪpi/
recover /rɪ'kʌvə/
split up with someone /split 'ʌp
  wɪð ˌsʌmwʌn/
stick up for /stɪk 'ʌp fə/
tolerate /'tɒləreɪt/
turn a blind eye /ˌtɜːn ə blaɪnd
  'aɪ/
unattractive /ʌnə'træktɪv/
windsurfing /'wɪndsɜːfɪŋ/

Issue eight
part two
aggression /əˈgreʃn/
blast out /blɑːst ˈaʊt/
alertness /əˈlɜːtnəs/
basket /ˈbɑːskɪt/
cause (v) /kɔːz/
discordant /dɪsˈkɔːdənt/
depressing /dɪˈpresɪŋ/
formal /ˈfɔːməl/
harmonious /hɑːˈməʊnɪəs/
harsh /hɑːʃ/
headphones /ˈhedfəʊnz/
help yourself /ˈhelp jɔːˈself/
hiss (v) /hɪs/
jealousy /ˈdʒeləsi/
joyful /ˈdʒɔɪfl/
moonlight /ˈmuːnlaɪt/
peaceful /ˈpiːsfl/
promote /prəˈməʊt/
resistance /rɪˈzɪstəns/
soothing /ˈsuːðɪŋ/
speed (v) /spiːd/
stereo /ˈsterɪəʊ/
stimulating /ˈstɪmjʊleɪtɪŋ/
subjective /sʌbˈdʒektɪv/
sun cream /ˈsʌn kriːm/
taste (v) /teɪst/
thunder (v) /ˈθʌndə/
traditional /trəˈdɪʃənl/
tranquillizers /ˈtræŋkwɪˌlaɪzəz/
violent /ˈvaɪələnt/

Issue eight
part three
abuse (n) /əˈbjuːs/
atmosphere /ˈætməsfɪə(r)/
celebrate /ˈseləbreɪt/
court (n) /kɔːt/
effectively /ɪˈfektɪvli/
foul (n) /faʊl/
hug (v) /hʌg/
kick-off /ˈkɪk ɒf/
kit /kɪt/
opponent /əˈpəʊnənt/
portable /ˈpɔːtəbl/
poster /ˈpəʊstə(r)/
queue /kjuː/
release (v) /rɪˈliːs/
roar (v) /rɔː(r)/
scream (v) /skriːm/
sequence /ˈsiːkwəns/
slogan /ˈsləʊgən/
stadium /ˈsteɪdɪəm/
wig /wɪg/

Issue nine
part one
accomplished /əˈkʌmplɪʃt/
Air Force /ˈeə fɔːs/
avalanche /ˈævəlɑːntʃ/
bury /ˈberi/
camp (n) /kæmp/
challenge /ˈtʃælɪndʒ/
climber /ˈklaɪmə/

commander /kəˈmɑːndə/
continent /ˈkɒntɪnənt/
drift (v) /drɪft/
essential /ɪˈsenʃl/
exceptionally /ekˈsepʃənli/
expedition /ekspəˈdɪʃn/
explorer /eksˈplɔːrə(r)/
extensively /ekstensɪvli/
incident /ˈɪnsɪdənt/
Islamic /ɪzˈlæmɪk/
melting /ˈmeltɪŋ/
polar /ˈpəʊlə/
polar bear /ˈpəʊlə beə(r)/
possibility /ˌpɒsɪˈbɪlɪti/
radio (v) /ˈreɪdɪəʊ/
satellite /ˈsætəlaɪt/
secret /ˈsiːkrət/
space shuttle /ˈspeɪs ʃʌtl/
supplies (n) /səˈplaɪz/
surprising /səˈpraɪzɪŋ/
track (n) /træk/
universe /ˈjuːnɪvɜːs/
unsupported /ˌʌnsəˈpɔːtɪd/

Issue nine
part two
back-stage /ˈbæk ˈsteɪdʒ/
cough /kɒf/
cut down /kʌt ˈdaʊn/
delighted (adj) /dɪˈlaɪtɪd/
fantastic /fænˈtæstɪk/
foolish /ˈfuːlɪʃ/
headgear /ˈhedgɪə(r)/
hurtle /ˈhɜːtl/
imagine /ɪˈmædzɪn/
introduce /ˌɪntrəˈdjuːs/
lottery /ˈlɒtəri/
misconception /ˌmɪskənˈsepʃn/
obliged /əˈblaɪdʒd/
outcome /ˈaʊtkʌm/
out of control /ˌaʊt əv kənˈtrəʊl/
paralysed /ˈpærəlaɪzd/
protective /prəˈtektɪv/
risk /rɪsk/
seat belt /ˈsiːt belt/
share (n) /ʃeə/
skid /skɪd/
steep /stiːp/
track (n) /træk/
variety /vəˈraɪəti/
woodland /ˈwʊdlənd/

Issue nine
part three
archery /ˈɑːtʃəri/
badminton /ˈbædmɪntən/
career /kəˈrɪə(r)/
compete /kəmˈpiːt/
discipline /ˈdɪsəplɪn/
eating disorders /ˈiːtɪŋ dɪsˌɔːdəz/
emphasis /ˈemfəsɪs/
fair play /feə ˈpleɪ/
fencing /ˈfensɪŋ/
gymnastics /dʒɪmˈnæstɪks/

honesty /ˈɒnɪsti/
illustrate /ˈɪləstreɪt/
obscene /əbˈsiːn/
Olympics /əˈlɪmpɪks/
stunted (adj) /ˈstʌntɪd/
training /ˈtreɪnɪŋ/
volleyball /ˈvɒlibɔːl/
wrestling /ˈreslɪŋ/

Songbook
sacrifice /ˈsækrɪfaɪs/
search your soul /ˌsɜːtʃ jɔː ˈsəʊl/
walk the wire /ˌwɔːk ðə ˈwaɪə(r)/
worth /wɜːθ/

Issue ten
part one
astonished /əˈstɒnɪʃt/
astrology /əˈstrɒlədʒi/
background /ˈbækgraʊnd/
complimentary /kɒmpləˈmentri/
consult /kənˈsʌlt/
feedback /ˈfiːdbæk/
graphology /grəˈfɒlədʒi/
handwriting /ˈhændraɪtɪŋ/
horoscope /ˈhɒrəskəʊp/
moral /ˈmɒrəl/
particularly /pəˈtɪkjələli/
predict /prɪˈdɪkt/
procedure /prəsiːdʒə(r)/
psychologist /saɪˈkɒləˌdʒɪst/
religion /rəˈlɪdʒn/
rubbish /ˈrʌbɪʃ/
specific /spəˈsɪfɪk/
value /ˈvæljuː/

Issue ten
part two
abroad /əˈbrɔːd/
adventure /ədˈventʃə(r)/
award (v) /əˈwɔːd/
boring /ˈbɔːrɪŋ/
budget /ˈbʌdʒɪt/
charge (v) /tʃɑːdʒ/
community service /kəˈmjuːnɪti ˌsɜːvɪs/
construction /kənˈstrʌkʃn/
decision /dɪˈsɪʒn/
engineering /ˌendʒəˈnɪərɪŋ/
gap year /ˈgæp jɪə(r)/
graduate (v) /ˈgrædjueɪt/
homeless /ˈhəʊmləs/
homesickness /ˈhəʊmˌsɪknəs/
independent /ˌɪndɪˈpendənt/
industry /ˈɪndəstri/
initiative /ɪˈnɪʃətɪv/
instinctively /ɪnˈstɪŋkˌtɪvli/
library /ˈlaɪbrəri/
loneliness /ˈləʊnliˌnəs/
medicine /ˈmedsn, -ɪsn/
poorer /ˈpɔːrə(r)/
promptly /ˈprɒmptli/
put in charge of /ˌpʊt ɪn ˈtʃɑːdʒ əv/
qualified (adj) /ˈkwɒlɪfaɪd/
school-leaver /ˈskuːl ˌliːvə(r)/

schoolroom /ˈskuːlrʊm/
service /ˈsɜːvɪs/
solo /ˈsəʊləʊ/
stayed still /steɪd ˈstɪl/
sympathetic /sɪmpəˈθetɪk/
temporary /ˈtempəˌreri/
Third World /ˈθɜːd ˈwɜːld/
tight /taɪt/
tummy upsets /ˈtʌmi ˌʌpset/
waste (n) /weɪst/

Issue ten
part three
acoustic guitar /əˌkuːstɪk gɪˈtɑː(r)/
amplifier /ˈæmplɪfaɪə(r)/
body piercing /ˈbɒdi ˌpɪəsɪŋ/
drum kit /ˈdrʌm kɪt/
instrument /ˈɪnstrəˌmənt/
lyrics /ˈlɪrɪks/
microphone /ˈmaɪkrəfəʊn/
mini skirt /ˈmɪni ˌskɜːt/
mixing desk /ˈmɪksɪŋ desk/
saxophone /ˈsæksəˌfəʊn/
society /səˈsaɪəti/
trumpet /ˈtrʌmpɪt/

Issue eleven
part one
bellow (v) /ˈbeləʊ/
blind date /blaɪnd ˈdeɪt/
die of embarassment /daɪ əv ɪmˈbærəsmənt/
grumble (v) /ˈgrʌmbl/
impressed /ɪmˈprest/
insensitive /ɪnˈsensətɪv/
insist /ɪnˈsɪst/
mumble /ˈmʌmbl/
mutter /ˈmʌtə/
pick someone up /ˌpɪk sʌmwɒn ˈʌp/
popcorn /ˈpɒpkɔːn/
snob /snɒb/
suggest /səˈdʒest/
whisper (v) /ˈwɪspə(r)/

Issue eleven
part two
basically /ˈbeɪsɪkli/
degree /dɪˈgriː/
fitness programme /ˈfɪtnəs ˌprəʊgræm/
give something up /ˌgɪv sʌmθɪŋ ˈʌp/
gym /ˌdʒɪm/
hide behind /ˌhaɪd bɪˈhaɪnd/
intend /ɪnˈtend/
kick boxing /ˈkɪk ˌbɒksɪŋ/
middle class /ˈmɪdl ˌklɑːs/
pile /paɪl/
possession /pəˈzeʃn/
prejudice /ˈpredʒədɪs/
primitive /ˈprɪmɪtɪv/
qualification /ˌkwɒlɪfɪˈkeɪʃn/
quit /kwɪt/

tournament /'tɔ:nəmənt/
unlikely /ʌn'laɪkli/

Issue eleven
part three
abruptly /ə'brʌptli/
acceptable /æk'septɪbl/
apologetically /ə'pɒlə,dʒetɪkli/
bowl /bəʊl/
brake (n) /breɪk/
confusion /kən'fju:ʒn/
crash (n) /kræʃ/
doubtfully /'daʊtfəli/
exclaim /eks'kleɪm/
guest /gest/
hopelessly /'həʊpləsli/
host /həʊst/
hurry /'hʌri/
image /'ɪmɪdʒ/
irregular /ɪ'regjələ(r)/
mechanically /mə'kænɪkli/
mysteriously /mɪs'tɪəriəsli/
nonsense /'nɒnsəns/
reflection /rɪ'flekʃn/
rudely /'ru:dli/
ruined /'ru:ɪnd/
sigh (v) /saɪ/
steady /'stedi/
teapot /'ti:pɒt/
uneven /ʌn'i:vn/
window-pane /'wɪndəʊ ,peɪn/

Songbook
faith /feɪθ/
forever /fər'evə(r)/
see someone through something
  /,si: sʌmwɒn 'θru: sʌmθɪŋ/
see the best in
  someone/something /,si: ðə
  'best ɪn sʌmwɒn/sʌmθɪŋ/
stand by someone /stænd 'baɪ
  ,sʌmwɒn/
stand tall /stænd 'tɔ:l/
thankful /'θæŋkfl/

Issue twelve
part one
ambition /æm'bɪʃn/
appeal (v) /ə'piəl/
bend down (v) /bend 'daʊn/
biro /'baɪrəʊ/
calculator /'kælkjʊleɪtə(r)/
collar /'kɒlə(r)/
consideration /kənsɪdə'reɪʃn/
fortune /'fɔ:tʃu:n/
gadget /'gædʒɪt/
gas /gæs/
gramophone /'græməfəʊn/
invention /ɪn'venʃn/
inventor /ɪn'ventə/
light bulb /'laɪt bʌlb/
luminous /'lu:mɪnəs/
motor-powered /'məʊtə
  ,paʊəd/
patent /'peɪtənt/
professional /prə'feʃnl/

radioactive /'reɪdɪəʊ,æktɪv/
reject (v) /rə'dʒekt/
slippers /'slɪpəz/
solution /sə'lu:ʃn/
spectacles /'spektəklz/
stethoscope /'steθəskəʊp/
submarine /'sʌbməri:n/
talent /'tælənt/
thoroughly /'θʌrəli/
turn down /'tɜ:n 'daʊn/

Issue twelve
part two
analysis /ə'næləsɪs/
assistant /ə'sɪstənt/
assumption /ə'sʌmpʃn/
channel hop /'tʃænl hɒp/
chat show /'tʃæt ʃəʊ/
commercial /kə'mɜ:ʃl/
concentrate /'kɒnsəntreɪt/
dishonesty /dɪs'ɒnɪsti/
documentary /,dɒkju'mentri/
dreadful /'dredfʊl/
engage /ɪn'geɪdʒ/
executive /ɪg'zekjətɪv/
get on someone's nerves /get
  ɒn 'sʌmwɒnz ,nɜ:vs/
glued to a set /,glu:d tu: ə 'set/
indifference /ɪn'dɪfrəns/
insight /'ɪnsaɪt/
laundry /'lɔ:ndri/
media /'mi:dɪə/
receptive /rɪ'septɪv/
repeat (n) /rəpi:t/
resign /rɪ'zaɪn/
situation comedy /sɪtʃʊ,eɪʃn
  'kɒmədi/
soap /səʊp/
system /'sɪstəm/
topic /'tɒpɪk/
viewer /'vju:ə/
wallpaper /'wɔ:lpeɪpə(r)/

Issue twelve
part three
apartment /ə'pɑ:tmənt/
bowling alley /'bəʊlɪŋ ,æli/
bungalow /'bʌŋgələʊ/
cottage /'kɒtɪdʒ/
derelict /'derə,lɪkt/
entertainment complex
  /entə'teɪnmənt ,kɒmpleks/
high-rise /'haɪ raɪz/
hut /hʌt/
luxurious /lʌg'ʒʊəriəs/
mansion /'mænʃn/
mugged /mʌgd/
multi-screen cinema /'mʌlti
  skri:n 'sɪnəmə/
old-fashioned /əʊld 'fæʃnd/
pollution /pə'lu:ʃn/
single-storey /sɪŋgl 'stɔ:ri/